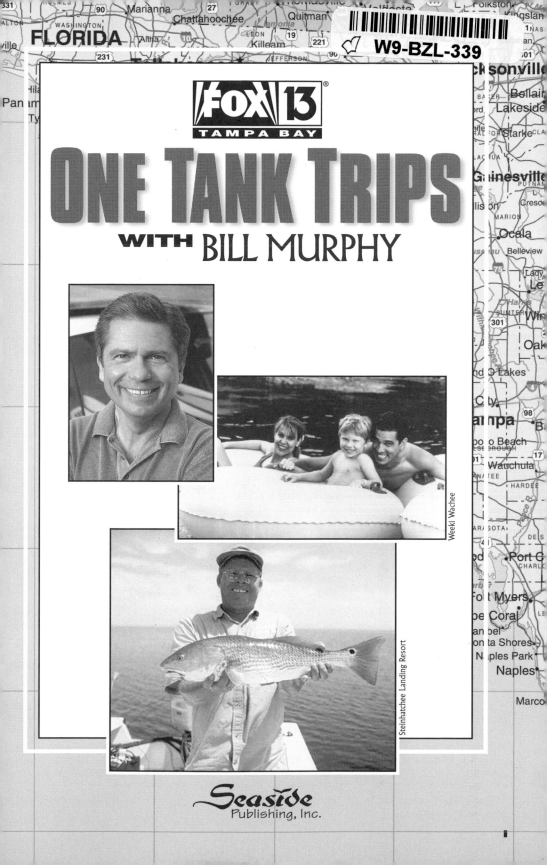

FOX 13
TAMPA BAY

ONE TANK TRIPS

WITH BILL MURPHY

Weeki Wachee

Steinhatchee Landing Resort

Seaside
Publishing, Inc.

Publisher
Joyce LaFray

Senior Editor
Vicki Krueger

Design & Illustration
James Wahl
Kim Kehoe
Kevin Coccaro

Additional copies of this book may be ordered by calling:

1-888-ONE-TANK
or 1-888-663-8265

Or, you may write the Publisher at:

Publishing, Inc.
P. O. Box 14441
St. Petersburg, FL 33733

Visit Our Website and order online at: **famousflorida.com**
E-mail: **sales@famousflorida.com**
Manufactured in the United States of America
ISBN: 0-942084-24-1

12th Printing
Library of Congress Catalog Number: 99 075770

©*1999 New World Communications of Tampa, Inc.*

Special thanks for photos and information: Geiger & Associates; Dean Fowler, Steinhatchee Landing Resort.

Front cover photos: Dan Gaye/Studio 75   **Back cover photos:** Bill Murphy; Dan Gaye/Studio 75, Crystal River Manatee, Geiger & Associates; Sunset, © Lee Island Coast; Lighthouse on Lake Dora, © 1997 C. J. Jean.

Special Sales: Bulk purchases (12+ copies) for **FOX13 TAMPA BAY'S ONE TANK TRIPS WITH BILL MURPHY** are available to companies at special discounts. For more information call: **1-888-ONE-TANK [663-8265)** or write to: Special Sales Seaside Publishing, Inc. 811 42nd Street South, St. Petersburg, FL 33711

While we have been very careful to assure the accuracy of the information in this guide, time brings change, and, consequently, the publisher cannot accept responsibility for errors which may occur. All prices and opening times are based on information given to us at press time. Admission fees and hours may change, so be sure to call ahead. We welcome tips for inclusion in future editions, comments and suggestions.

Dedication

This book is dedicated to my co-workers at **FOX13** — a remarkably talented group. In particular, the "photogs" whose beautiful pictures helped me so much to tell these stories; and to Lee Barrett, videotape editor extraordinaire who put all the pieces together.

Also, my thanks to you, the **FOX13** viewer, who over the years has been so gracious in allowing me into your home to spin my yarns.

And, of course, to my family for their love and support.

Acknowledgments

One Tank Trips reflects the contributions of countless people. First, a huge thank you to the producers, editors, designers, photographers and the team at **FOX13**. Their guidance and assistance have been invaluable. This book would not have been possible without the special efforts of:

David Boylan, Vice President, General Manager

Philip Metlin, Vice President, News Director

James Wahl, Design Director

Kim Kehoe, Senior Designer

Cynthia Lynn Landers, Executive Producer, FOX13 Good Day Tampa Bay

Carrie Schroeder, Promotion/Publicity Manager

A special thanks to:

Vicki Krueger, Senior Editor, Seaside Publishing, Inc.

Carolyn Forrest, Vice President, FTS

And:

Chrysler and Jeep Dealers

CONTENTS

CONTENTS

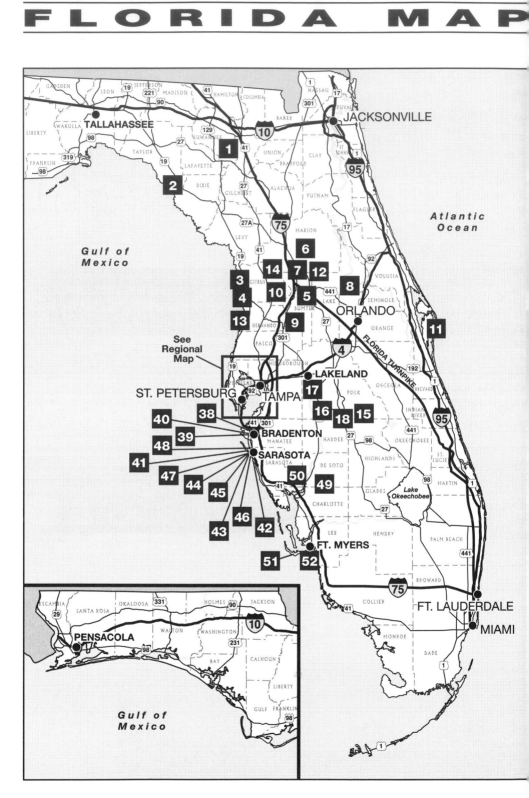

One Tank Trips

NORTH FLORIDA

1 Ginnie Springs Resort
2 Steinhatchee Scallop Dive

CENTRAL FLORIDA

3 Crystal River
4 Homosassa Springs
   State Wildlife Park
5 Lakeridge Winery
6 Marjorie Kinnan Rawlings Site
7 Micanopy
8 Mount Dora
9 Pioneer Florida Museum
10 Rogers' Christmas
   House & Village
11 Ron Jon Surf Shop
12 Silver Springs
13 Weeki Wachee Springs
14 Wild Bill's Airboat Tours

Polk County

15 Bok Tower Gardens
16 Cypress Gardens
17 International Sport
   Aviation Museum
18 Spook Hill

WEST CENTRAL FLORIDA

Hillsborough County

19 Daytime Ybor City
20 Hillsborough River State Park
21 Lowry Park Zoo
22 The Florida Aquarium

Pinellas County

23 Bill Jackson
   Shop for Adventure
24 Boyd Hill Nature Park
25 Captain Memo's Pirate Cruise
26 Clearwater Marine Aquarium
27 Fort De Soto Park
28 Gulfport Gallery Walk
29 Haslam's Book Store
30 Heritage Village
31 Museum of Fine Arts
32 Pass-A-Grille
33 Salvador Dali Museum
34 Sawgrass Lake Park
35 Tarpon Springs
36 Ted Peters Famous Smoked Fish
37 The Pier

Manatee County

38 Gamble Plantation State Historic Site
39 Linger Lodge R.V. Resort & Restaurant
40 South Florida Museum
   Bishop Planetarium
   Parker Manatee Aquarium

Sarasota County

41 Ca' d'Zan, Ringling Residence
42 Historic Spanish Point
43 Marie Selby Botanical Gardens
44 Mote Marine Aquarium
45 St. Armands Circle
46 Sarasota Bay Explorers
47 Sarasota Classic Car Museum
48 Sarasota Jungle Gardens

SOUTHWEST FLORIDA

49 Arcadia
50 Canoe Outpost at Peace River
51 Captiva Island
52 Edison-Ford Winter Estates

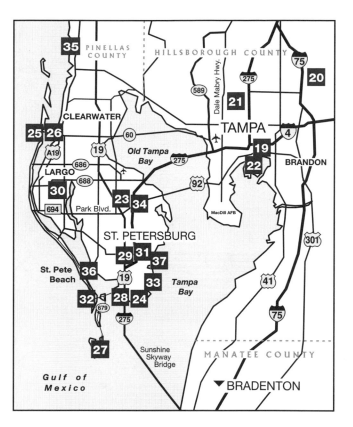

Discover the *real* Florida

We always enjoy watching Bill Murphy and **FOX13** take us to unique travel spots off the beaten path. The Chrysler and Jeep dealers really appreciate Bill's efforts to share these not-to-be missed experiences. And his trips help us plan our own outings in the Tampa Bay area.

Whether you are headed to the historic town of Micanopy to hunt for antiques, to Wild Bill's for an exciting airboat ride, or to Tarpon Springs to watch the famous Greek cross ceremony, you will want to experience a comfortable ride. Our 27 dealerships are available to provide you with the best transportation to your chosen destination. Stop in and see us.

This handy travel guide is a must for those with an unrelenting wanderlust for discovering the real Florida. It contains all the information you need for an enjoyable outing, including travel tips and detailed maps for each trip. For quick access, keep it in your glove compartment. You will soon find it to be a necessity!

These **FOX13 One Tank Trips** have always been a part of our Chrysler and Jeep family, and we know they will become a part of yours.

Your Chrysler and Jeep Dealers

A Word From FOX13

I hope you enjoy using this book as much as we have enjoyed putting it together. It has been a pleasure to take a fresh look at the unique adventures and attractions that are just a tank of gas away.

There are many on our team who deserve credit for contributing their efforts to this book. At the top of my list are the switchboard operators at **FOX13**. They are the ones who made me aware of the numerous calls we get at the station every time one of our **One Tank Trip** episodes airs. They told me that viewers wanted information on the trips, including directions, phone numbers and admission prices. The obvious solution was to compile this handy travel guide.

I hope that this is the first of many editions of a very special guide that showcases the fun and fascinating, educational and entertaining places in our Sunshine State. Enjoy the book and be sure to watch **FOX13** for your next **One Tank Trip**.

David Boylan
Vice President and General Manager
FOX13

Bill Murphy is a veteran TV news reporter and anchor who has spent nearly 15 years in Tampa Bay broadcasting. He is the host of **FOX13**'s popular series of feature reports, **One Tank Trips**, which spotlight one-of-a-kind destinations that take one tank of gas or less to reach. He also serves as weekend anchor of **FOX13 Good Day Tampa Bay**.

After moving to the Tampa Bay area in 1985, Bill became host of the popular talk show "Murphy in the Morning," which received an Emmy nomination in 1991. With his unique blend of warmth and humor, Bill welcomed more than 3,000 guests to 1,600 shows during the program's successful six-and-a-half-year run.

Before he came to Florida, Bill's broadcast career included seven years as the anchor at KSBW-TV in Monterey, Calif., and stints at a television station in Seattle and radio stations in Palm Springs and Los Angeles.

When he's not watching the gas gauge and driving off on another intriguing **One Tank Trip**, Bill gets around on in-line skates, and also enjoys reading, tennis and handball.

A Word From Bill Murphy

It has been my great pleasure to take the viewers of **FOX13** to so many delightful attractions around the state. Florida may be known to the world as the home of theme parks, but I've found out there's so much more to discover and enjoy.

This handy guide is my chance to share with you some of my favorite and most memorable adventures. I hope you enjoy them as much as I have.

One bit of advice: We have checked and double-checked information, such as hours of operation, admission prices, websites and so on. But, please, please, please, call ahead anyway. Sometimes things do change. And when you get them on the phone, ask them about the weather.

When you use this book, and I hope you'll do that a lot, notice that it will stay open at the destination you've selected. We did that on purpose, with a special binding, to make this guide as user-friendly as possible.

Finally, let me hear from you! I'd love to know your impressions of these **One Tank Trips**. And if you have suggestions for future journeys, I'd love to hear about those, too.

Happy trails to you!

Bill

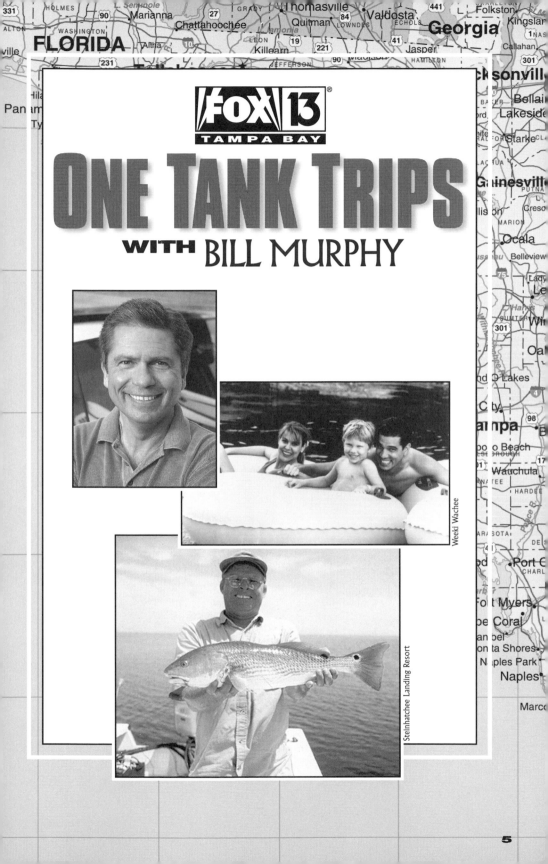

FOX 13
TAMPA BAY

ONE TANK TRIPS

WITH BILL MURPHY

Weeki Wachee

Steinhatchee Landing Resort

Ginnie Springs Resort

Outdoor Adventure Awaits

© Glenda Jones

© William Dooley

The clear water of Ginnie Springs will bring out the adventurer in you.

The trip

If Ginnie Springs doesn't have it all, it sure comes close. And the setting is simply gorgeous! A leisurely float down the Santa Fe River will calm the savage beast in you.

What to see

The crystal-clear water in the springs is perfect for scuba diving. Cavern-diving and cave-diving are available for the experienced and adventurous diver.

Other highlights

Go canoeing, tubing, snorkeling and hiking. This is the perfect day with Mother Nature. And if you want to stay awhile, nothing beats camping at Ginnie Springs Resort. Set on more than 200 acres of unspoiled central Florida forest, this privately owned resort offers 55 campsites with electric and water hook-ups, heated bathrooms, picnic tables and grills and a well-stocked general store.

The facts

7300 N.E. Ginnie Springs Road
High Springs, FL 32643
(904) 454-2202

Admission: *General daily admission is $7 for adults, $3 for ages 7-14, free for ages 6 and younger. Call for daily admission for scuba diving, camping and cottage rentals and camp/dive packages.*

Hours: *Open Monday-Thursday in the summer from 8 a.m. to 7 p.m., 8 a.m. to 6 p.m. in the winter. Open Sunday in the summer from 8 a.m. to 10 p.m., 8 a.m. to 7 p.m. in the winter. Open year-round on Friday and Saturday from 8 a.m. to 10 p.m.*

www.ginniesprings.com

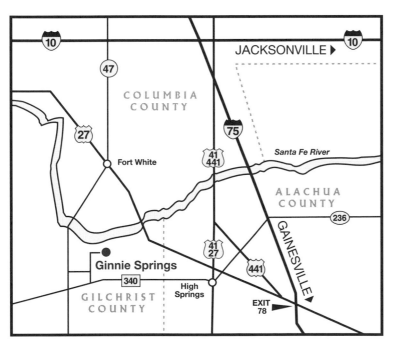

Directions

From Interstate 75, take Exit 78 west to High Springs. At the light in High Springs turn left onto U.S. 41 & U.S. 27. Go south through town to County Road 340. Turn right on C.R. 340 and go west about six miles. Ginnie Springs is on the right.

"Jacques Cousteau said of his visit to the waters of Ginnie Springs: 'Visibility forever!' He was right."

Steinhatchee Scallop Dive

Nature's Bounty

Steinhatchee Landing Resort

No matter how you cook your catch, Florida scallops are a taste treat.

Bill gets ready to sample his catch.

The trip

Along the winding backroads of northern Florida, you'll find this tiny fishing village. The catch of the summer — bay scallops.

What to see

Before you get in the water, you'll need to get a saltwater license. They cost $14 and if you don't get one before you go to Steinhatchee you can get one at any of the marinas there. To find the scallops, you'll need a pair of fins, a mask and a snorkel. As a first-time scalloper, I find it has nothing to do with fishing. It's all about gathering. However, there are some limits on how much you gather. The law lets you take two gallons per person per trip.

A bumper crop of scallops nestles in the shallow waters where the Steinhatchee River meets the Gulf of Mexico. The vast underworld of sea grass is fertile ground for scallops. Some are easy to find. Others are more elusive. But don't worry, they don't bite.

Then it's time to shuck your catch. Maybe you'll discover you have a natural talent for prying open the shells. Once you're done, you can cook your catch. Broiled or fried, there's nothing better than cooking up fresh Florida scallops.

The facts

Steinhatchee Landing Resort
Highway 51 N.
Steinhatchee, FL 32359
(800) 584-1709

Admission: *Free*

Hours: *Scallop season varies. It's usually from the beginning of July to mid-September. Call the resort to check.*

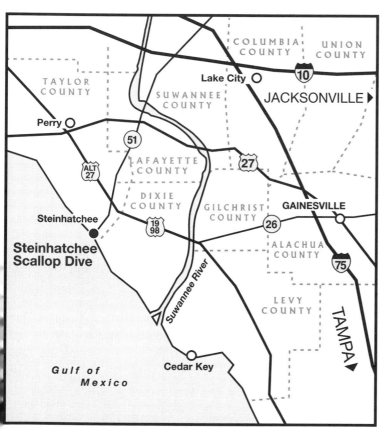

Directions

From Interstate 75, take the Brooksville exit and follow U.S. 98 north to U.S. 19. Follow U.S. 19 north to Taylor County. Take S.R. 51 in Taylor County west to Steinhatchee.

"A fun day you'll remember long after the sun goes down."

▼
3

Crystal River
Swim with the Manatees

Up Close with the Gentle Giants

The Crystal River area is famous around the world as a haven for manatees.

The trip

Swimming with the manatees is something I'd wanted to do for a long time. My daughter Jessica and I finally had the chance when we visited Crystal River in Citrus County.

What to see

The best time of year to see manatees begins in October and ends in March. That's when water in the Gulf of Mexico is coolest, so the manatees head to the warm spring water near Kings Bay. Make sure you go early in the morning. Manatees are more likely to be around at that time.

Our guide was Diana Oestreich, the co-owner of Birds Underwater, a dive shop that offers manatee tours. She will tell you how to make friends with the sea giants.

Manatees have no natural enemies, so they aren't aggressive. And they are incredibly playful. They will roll on their backs so you can rub their stomachs. Sometimes they'll even grab your hand with a flipper because they want you to stay and play with them.

The facts

Birds Underwater Dive Shop
320 N.W. U.S. 19
Crystal River, FL 34428
(352) 563-2763 or (800)771-2763

Admission: *Call for tour and equipment rental rates.*
Hours: *Call for dive times, tour availability and reservations.*

www.birdsunderwater.com

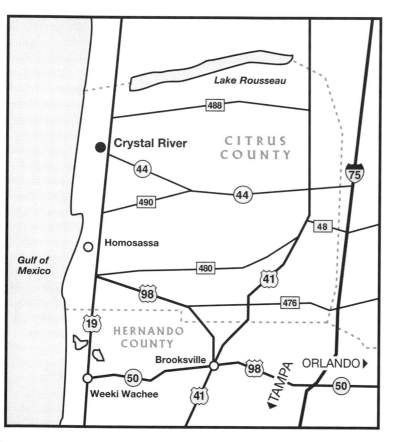

Directions

From Interstate 75, exit on U.S. 98 west, which will take you to U.S. 19. Head north on U.S. 19 toward Crystal River. Birds Underwater is half a mile north of County Road 44 on the south side of the road, behind Dockside Trading Co.

"An experience you will never forget."

Homosassa Springs State Wildlife Park

Fall in Love with the Manatees

© Homosassa Springs State Wildlife Park

© Homosassa Springs State Wildlife Park

From a pontoon boat or observation deck, you can see the manatees, deer, birds and other wildlife that make Homosassa Springs their home.

The trip

Just off U.S.19, away from the cars and strip malls, sits a natural treasure. Let a pontoon boat take you up Homosassa River and back to the "real" Florida. At the headwater of the river sits this 166-acre park, preserving and protecting Florida wildlife.

What to see

What a perfect place to see manatees! The Manatee Education Center is a halfway house for those who have been injured by boat propellers. They'll recover here until they're well enough to be released. Through the park's underwater observatory, you get to see these gentle giants and a rich variety of other marine life.

Other highlights

Enjoy the sights and sounds of nature in the park that animals have made their home. Trails offer glimpses of deer, bear, bobcats and a variety of native birds. There's also a great little gift shop.

The facts

4150 S. Suncoast Blvd.
Homosassa, FL 34446
(352) 628-2311

Admission: *$7.95 adults, $4.95 ages 3-12, free for children younger than 3.*

Hours: *Open daily 9 a.m. to 5:30 p.m. Ticket sales end at 4 p.m.*

www.citrusdirectory.com/hsswp

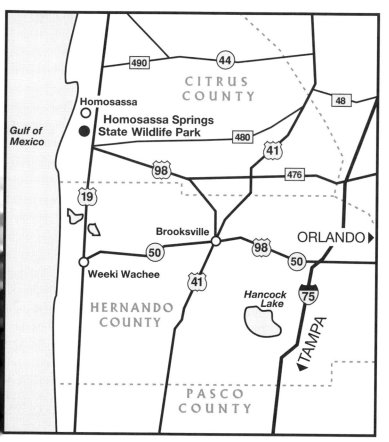

"Escape the real Florida of today for the real Florida of days gone by."

Directions

From Interstate 75, exit on U.S. 98 west, which will take you to U.S. 19. Head north on U.S. 19. The visitor center and main entrance to Homosassa Springs State Wildlife Park is on U.S. 19 in Homosassa Springs.

Lakeridge Winery & Vineyards

A Taste of the Sweet Life

Lakeridge Winery makes its wines from grapes developed to grow in Florida's climate.

The trip

What a wonderful surprise this place is! Florida's largest winery and vineyards overlooks the rolling hills of south Lake County. And the Spanish-style Lakeridge Winery building is beautiful.

What to see

Your visit will begin with a tour of the winery and a look at the vineyards. You'll learn that (with all due respect to California and New York) the first recorded reference to wine made from grapes from the New World was to those grown near Jacksonville.

After the tour, it's time to do some tasting. Lakeridge has won many awards for its wines. Right now it produces several very good whites and one red, most on the sweet side.

Other highlights

In the gift shop you can buy wine and wine-related items — wine glasses, corkscrews and even clothing celebrating wine! For the kids, there's free grape juice and cartoons. There's also a picnic area. So bring along some cheese and the romantic in you, and enjoy the sweeter side of life.

The facts

19239 U.S. 27 N.
Clermont, FL 34711
(352) 394-8627 or
(800) 768-WINE(9463)

Admission: *Free*

Hours: *Open Monday through Saturday 10 a.m. to 5 p.m., Sunday 11 a.m. to 5 p.m. Closed on major holidays.*

www.lakeridgewinery.com

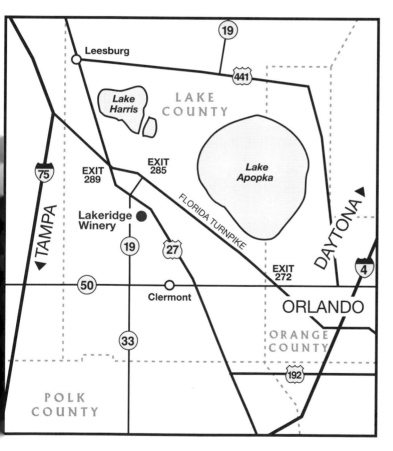

Directions

From Interstate 75, take the Route 50 exit east to U.S. 27. On U.S. 27, go north to the winery. From Interstate 4, take the U.S. 27 exit and go north to the winery.

"This place is very 'tasteful.' Get it?"

Marjorie Kinnan Rawlings State Historic Site

A Place of Inspiration

Marjorie Kinnan Rawlings drew the inspiration for her books from her home at Cross Creek. A typewriter still sits on the veranda where she wrote.

Marjorie Kinnan Rawlings State Historic Site

The trip

"I don't know how anyone can live without some place of enchantment to turn to." For author Marjorie Kinnan Rawlings, that place was her home at Cross Creek.

What to see

This Cracker-style house and farm is where Marjorie Kinnan Rawlings wrote "The Yearling," a novel for which she won the Pulitzer Prize in 1939. Today you can still feel her presence as you tour the house and grounds. Step out on the veranda and take a deep breath. The air is full of the scents of pine and citrus that instilled her love for Florida. It's on this veranda, where her typewriter still sits, that she did most of her writing — inspired by the magic of this place.

Her words, from her book "Cross Creek," summarize her feelings best: "It seems to me that the earth may be borrowed but not bought. It may be used but not owned....we are tenants and not possessors, lovers and not masters."

The facts

Route 3, Box 92
Hawthorne, FL 32640
(352) 466-3672

Admission: *Farm yard and trails are free. Admission for the house tour is $3 adults, $2 ages 6-12, free for 5 and younger.*

Hours: *The house is open to the public only through tours on Thursday through Sunday. Tours are offered October through July; no tours are conducted in August and September. Call for a schedule of tour times. The yard, citrus grove and nature trails are open year-round from 9 a.m. to 5 p.m. daily and are free.*

www.flamuseums.org/fam /flamuseums/pages/050.htm

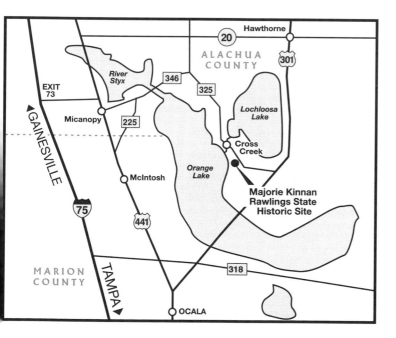

"The home and inspiration for a truly remarkable woman."

Directions

From Interstate 75 take Exit 73 (Micanopy) east to U.S. 441. Turn right on U.S. 441 and go about one mile to County Road 346. Turn left on C.R. 346 and go four or five miles to C.R. 325. Turn right on C.R. 325. The historical site is about four miles down C.R. 325 on the right.

Micanopy

Beauty Comes in Small Packages

The beautiful Herlong Mansion, with 12 bedrooms with private baths, is just one of the cozy bed and breakfasts in Micanopy.

The museum at Micanopy displays the five flags that have flown over Florida.

The trip

Just 20 minutes north of Ocala, you'll come upon the historic town of Micanopy, Florida's oldest inland settlement. The town's setting is one of beauty and charm. Named for Chief Micanopy, this little town is now one of the premier antique centers in the state.

What to see

In the mood for furniture, a cameo or a good book? You're sure to find just the thing in one of Micanopy's many antique and curio stores. Just strolling down the street makes you feel as though you've gone back to a simpler time.

Other highlights

All that shopping will make you hungry. Fortunately, there's great food here, whether you're in the mood for a quick sandwich, a scoop of ice cream or a full-fledged meal. And if you want to stay awhile, Micanopy has some wonderful bed and breakfasts.

The facts

*Micanopy Historical
Society Museum
607 N.E. First St.
P.O. Box 462
Micanopy, FL 32667
(352) 466-3200*

Admission: *Free*

Hours: *Stores are open daily, although some are closed
on Tuesdays. Most close on major holidays. Restaurant
hours vary.*

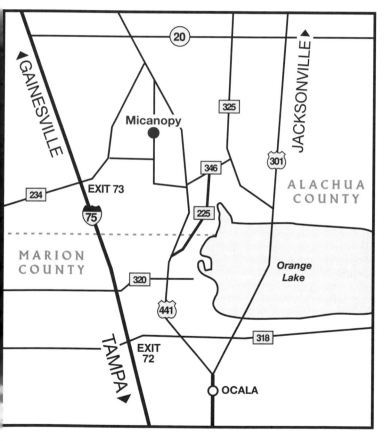

Directions

From Interstate 75, take Exit 73 and go 1 mile east to
downtown.

"Here's a
little piece
of the world
you can
enjoy for a
few hours
or for a
weekend
getaway."

Mount Dora

Treat Yourself to this Place

A horse-drawn carriage ride offers visitors a relaxed, open-air view of historic Mount Dora.

© 1997 C.J. Jean

This inland lighthouse was built in 1988 through resident donations.

© 1997 C.J. Jean

The trip

Mount Dora has been called many things: the New England of the South, the Antique Center of Central Florida and the City of Parks, among others. You can boat from Lake Dora all the way to the Atlantic, but as beautiful as this place is, why leave?

What to see

Nearly 50 gift shops, antique shops, art shops and boutiques call Mount Dora home. I call it "unique." Stop by Renninger's Antique Market. It has more than 700 vendors. On weekends, you can visit the indoor Flea Market next door to Renninger's.

Other highlights

You can't beat the parks in Mount Dora. The nature path at Palm Island Park leads you along the lake so you can enjoy nature's rich offerings. If you prefer beauty made by human hands, Mount Dora features some breathtaking buildings. Check out the Donnelly House. It displays Queen Anne architecture with a wrap-around porch and gingerbread trim. A night at the historic Lakeside Inn will be a memorable experience. And the Windsor Rose English Tea House offers a great cup of tea.

The facts

Mount Dora Area Chamber of Commerce
341 N. Alexander St.
Mount Dora, FL 32757
(352) 383-2165

Admission: *Free*
Hours: *Shop and restaurant hours vary.*

www.mt-dora.com

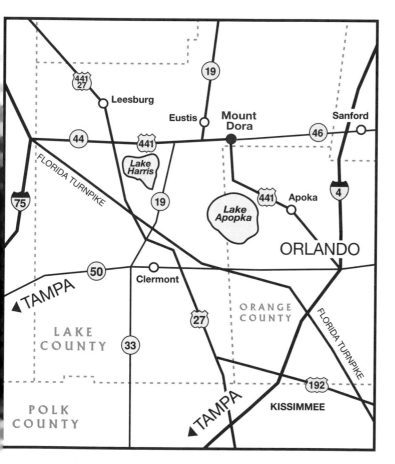

Directions

From Interstate 75, take County Road 44 to U.S. 441 east to Mount Dora. From Interstate 4, take U.S. 441 north to Mount Dora.

"As pretty a setting as anywhere in the state."

Pioneer Florida Museum

A Taste of Old Florida

The Lacoochee School has been restored and furnished to depict a one-room school house.

The trip

If you're not a fan of museums, don't let the word scare you. You'll spend happy hours here in buildings that let you experience life in Florida during the 1800s and early 1900s.

What to see

This place is a history buff's dream. Stop by the 1926 Lacoochee School and give the school bell a ring. Check out the office of Irvin S. Futch, turn-of-the-century dentist. Those instruments look scary! A trip to the Jack Bromley Shoe Repair Shop is good for the soul — not to mention the heel. Sorry.

Other highlights

See the collections of Native American artifacts, quilts, pottery and musical instruments. And don't miss the amazing collection of dolls depicting Florida's first ladies in their inaugural gowns.

The facts

15602 Pioneer Museum Road
Dade City, FL 33526
(352) 567-0262

Admission: *$5 adults, $4 ages 55 and older,*
$2 students 6-18, free for ages 5 and younger.

Hours: *Open Tuesday through Sunday 1-5 p.m.*
Closed on major holidays.

www.dadecity.com/museum

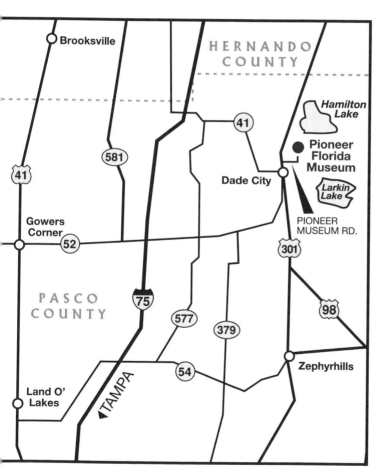

Directions

ioneer Museum Road is one mile north of Dade City on
U.S. 301.

"Young Floridians will enjoy this look at old Florida."

Rogers' Christmas House & Village

Jingle All the Way!

From displays of collectibles to decorations, the five houses here are packed with Christmas cheer.

The trip

It's time to hop aboard the holiday express! January or December or anytime in between, Rogers' Christmas House is a beautiful way t spend the holidays.

What to see

This village of five houses started as a gift shop in the early 1950s Now you can buy everything from decorations to linens and gourme food — as long as it involves that jolly bearded guy. Make sure yo stroll through all of the houses and the gardens outside.

You might want to select an ornament by Christopher Radko America's premier ornament designer. In fact, his ornaments can b seen on the White House Christmas tree every year.

Other highlights

Santa's list is here. Better check and see if you made it this year.

The facts

103 S. Saxon Ave.
Brooksville, FL 34601
(352) 796-2415

Admission: *Free*

Hours: *Open daily 9:30 a.m. to 5 p.m.*
Closed Christmas.

www.rogerschristmashouse.com

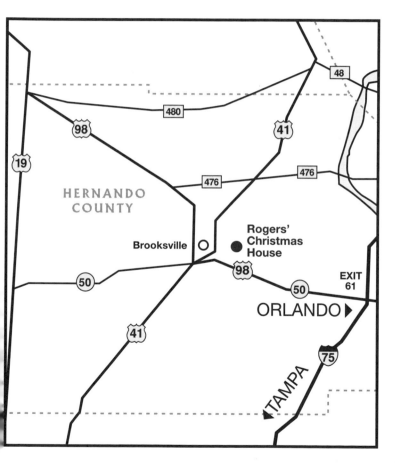

Directions

From Interstate 75 take the Brooksville/Ridge Manor take exit (Exit 61) west to Brooksville. That road becomes U.S. 50. Follow it about 10 miles to Brooksville. Rogers' Christmas House Village will be on the right.

"It's Christmas whenever you visit."

Ron Jon Surf Shop

Not Your Father's Surf Shop

Ron Ton Surf Shop

The exterior of Ron Jon's flagship store pays tribute to the beach lifestyle through photos and sand sculptures. Inside, you'll find all the accessories you could need for a beach visit.

The trip

Head east from the Tampa Bay area, and you'll see the billboards. You can't miss them along Interstate 4 as you head to Cocoa Beach. It's the "waterworld of eternal summer fun."

What to see

Need a T-shirt? At last count, they've sold more than 16 million. Ron Jon also sells shorts, swim suits, shoes and skirts. And check out the skateboards, sunblock and skis. (Most of their stuff begins with an "s," I guess.) Then there are the surfboards, skimboards, bodyboards and wakeboards. These folks are serious about their board knowledge. This place is huge! With 52,000 square feet, the store covers more than two acres. It's more of a palace than a surf shop. Visit once and you'll be hooked.

Other highlights

See the sculptures in the sports park outside the store. They're larger than life and worth a look. Or shop at the Ron Jon Beach Outpost and Ron Jon Watersports. Forget something? Ron Jon rents in-line skates, beach bikes and other sporting equipment. And when you're tired after a hard day's ride, take a break at the Ron Jon Surf Café.

The facts

4151 N. Atlantic Ave.
Cocoa Beach, FL 32931
(407) 799-8888 or
(888) RJ SURFS (757-8737)

Admission: *Free*
Hours: *Open 24 hours a day, 365 days a year.*

www.ronjons.com

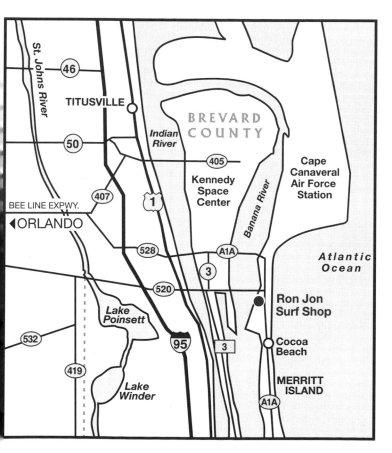

"A surfing experience that has nothing to do with changing channels on TV."

Directions

Drive eastbound from the Beeline Expressway (S.R. 528) or S.R. 520 east to Cocoa Beach. Ron Jon is at the corner of S.R. 520 and A1A, one minute from the Atlantic Ocean. From Interstate 95 take Exit 77B and go 16 miles east to S.R. 520 and A1A.

Silver Springs

A Florida Classic

© Silver Springs 1998

© Silver Springs 1998

Glass-bottom boats let passengers peer into the depths of the natural artesian springs. On dry land, you'll learn about the Florida panther in the Panther Prowl exhibit.

The trip

Florida's original attraction has been around since the 1870s and it's clear why — the crystal-clear spring water.

What to see

Since they were invented in 1878, the glass bottom boats of Silver Springs have fascinated millions. Looking down into the depths you can see the star of the show — the beautiful spring waters. These waters have been featured in a long list of movies and TV shows, including six "Tarzan" movies, two James Bond movies and the "Sea Hunt" TV show.

On a boat tour, you'll see the place where the monster emerged in the 1954 horror classic, "Creature from the Black Lagoon." On my tour, the boat captain said the creature still lived down there. I'm pretty sure I don't believe that. But looking down into that water makes me wonder...

Other highlights

Wildlife exhibits are everywhere. Panther Prowl lets you see a true Florida panther. World of Bears is the largest exhibit of its kind in the world. And don't forget the Lost River Voyage and the Jungle Cruise. There's also a special spot for children: Kids Ahoy! Playland features a Ferris wheel, fishing games and a playground, all on a replica of an 1800s riverboat.

The facts

5656 E. Silver Springs Blvd.
Silver Springs, FL 34488
(352) 236-2121 or (800) 234-7458

Admission: *$30.95 for adults, $21.95 for ages 3-10, free for ages 2 and younger. Discounts available.*

Hours: *Open Monday-Friday 10 a.m. to 5 p.m. Saturday-Sunday 9 a.m. to 5:30 p.m. Hours vary during summer and select holidays. Call for information.*

www.silversprings.com

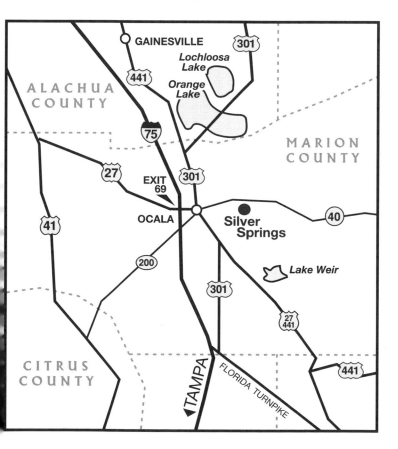

"This is a full day's worth of fun."

Directions

From Interstate 75, take Exit 69 (State Road 40) east 10 miles. Silver Springs will be on the right.

▼
13

Weeki Wachee Springs Waterpark

Mermaid Mania

© 1997 Weeki Wachee

Passengers on the Wilderness River Cruise can observe herons, otters, raccoons, osprey and endangered wood storks along the Weeki Wachee River.

© Weeki Wachee Spring

Weeki Wachee's famous mermaids perform every day in the underwater theater.

The trip

Weeki Wachee, home of those famous mermaids, is one of Florida's oldest theme parks. Now, the 200-acre waterpark includes water slides and boat rides, in addition to an underwater production of "The Little Mermaid."

What to see

Have you ever tried drinking a soft drink while wearing skates — under water? Weeki Wachee Springs' famous mermaids have done it. The mermaids have enchanted millions of visitors with their performances in the world's only underwater spring theater. One day, even Elvis Presley stopped by for a chat.

Other highlights

Another must-do is a trip along the enchanted river of the mermaids. Sit back and enjoy the natural beauty along the Weeki Wachee River. If thrills and spills are your speed, take the plunge into the spring water or zoom down the three-story waterslide.

The facts

6131 Commercial Way
Spring Hill, FL 34606
(352) 596-2062 or
(877) GO WEEKI (469-3354)

Admission: *$14.95 adults, $13.45 seniors,*
$10.95 ages 3-10, free for ages 2 and younger.
Prices adjusted seasonally from Labor Day through
March.

Hours: *Open 10 a.m. daily.*
Closing times vary. Hours vary during summer and
select holidays. Waterpark open seasonally. Call for
daily schedule.

www.weekiwachee.com

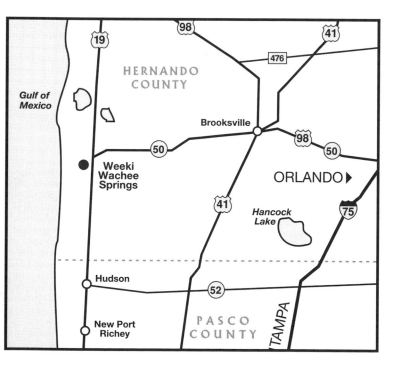

Directions

From Interstate 75, take Exit 61 (State Road 50) west
about 20 miles to U.S. 19. Weeki Wachee is at the intersection of U.S. 19 and S.R. 50 in Hernando County.

"An
old-fashioned
'theme park,'
a delightful
day."

Weeki Wachee Springs Waterpark

Wild Bill's Airboat Tours & Wildlife Preserve

Wild about Wild Bill's!

Airboats take visitors on a tour of the Withlacoochee River.

Animals at Wild Bill's include this white tiger.

© Karen Bender

Wild Bill's Airboat Tours & Wildlife Preserve

The trip

When your destination is Wild Bill's, be prepared. The wildlife are ready! The trip to the airboats includes a ride past Wild Bill's "babies" — lions and tigers and camels (oh my!) and more. This is one of my most favorite places!

What to see

It doesn't take long to realize this is going to be a beautiful voyage. Located on the Withlacoochee River, a ride on the Coast Guard-inspected airboats is a thrill. Welcome to gator country. On our visit, the gators were close enough to touch, but we didn't. And get a look at the wild boars, osprey, eagles, otters and deer.

Other highlights

Back on land, visit the wildlife park. You can pose with a puma and cuddle with a cub. Bill MacKay and his wife, Susie, have stories on each and every one.

The facts

12430 E. Gulf-to-Lake Highway
Inverness, FL 34450
(352) 726-6060

Admission: *$11.95 adults,*
$7.95 ages 11 and younger.

Hours: *Open daily 10 a.m. to 5 p.m.*
Closed Christmas.

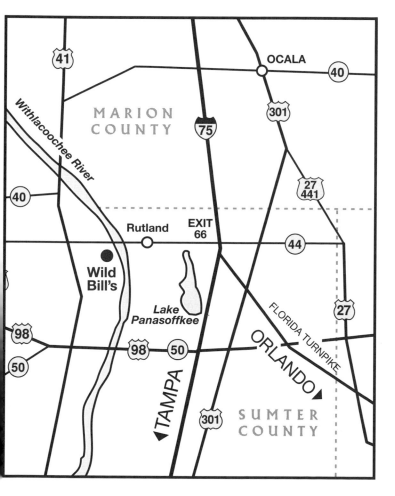

Directions

Take Interstate 75 to Exit 66 (Big Wildwood Truck Stop exit). Head west on State Road 44 for nine miles. Wild Bill's is on the left.

"The views are spectacular, the ride is exhilarating and the animals are so beautiful."

15

Bok Tower Gardens

Majestic Beauty

Bok Tower Gardens

The 157 acres of Bok Tower Gardens include flowering plants such as azaleas and camellias, along with ferns, palms, oaks and pines.

The carillon houses nearly 60 bronze bells.

The trip

Before he came to America, Edward Bok got this advice from his grandmother: "Make you the world a bit better or more beautiful because you have lived in it." Years later, author, publisher and Pulitzer Prize winner Edward Bok did just that. This is truly a place of beauty, and of peace, and of reflection.

What to see

The tower is built on peninsular Florida's highest point: elevation 298 feet. The detailed carvings on the 205-foot tower depict Florida's wildlife. The impressive brass door, depicting the creation of life, is shined once a month.

Other highlights

The tower houses one of the world's greatest carillons, making this a place of joyful music. You'll also need to stop by Pinewood House and Gardens, an example of an early Florida retreat estate. Stay at Chalet Suzanne, a gourmet retreat with European-styled rooms.

The facts

1151 Tower Blvd.
Lake Wales, FL 33853
(863) 676-9412 *(Recorded Information)*
(863) 676-1408 *(Administrative Offices)*

Admission: *$6 adults, $5 ages 62 and older, $2 ages 5-12, free for children younger than 5. Free until 9 a.m. on Saturday mornings.*

Hours: *Open daily 8 a.m. to 5 p.m. Call for a schedule of carillon concerts.*

www.boktower.org

FLORIDA TURNPIKE

75

27

4

Lake Buena Vista

LAKELAND

Lake Marion

17

Lake Pierce

17A

TAMPA

Bok Tower Gardens

60

Lake Wales

Tampa Bay

41

POLK COUNTY

"One of Florida's most beautiful settings. And the friendliest squirrels I've ever seen!"

Directions

Take U.S. 60 east to Lake Wales. At Buckmoore Road in Lake Wales, turn left and go up the hill to the blinking red light, which is Burns Avenue. Turn left on Burns Avenue. Bok Tower Gardens is up the hill on the right.

Cypress Gardens

Bring the Kids and Grandparents

© 1999 Florida Cypress Gardens Inc.

Cypress Gardens' Southern Belles stroll through the botanical beauty of this tropical showcase.

© 1999 Florida Cypress Gardens Inc.

The trip

Enter a whole new world at Cypress Gardens. Established in 1936, this exquisite park is Florida's first theme park. It's still a stunning place to visit!

What to see

Don't miss the variety of gardens. More than 200 couples a year take advantage of the splendor as a place to exchange wedding vows. The Botanical Gardens are a tropical paradise. Plantation Gardens are full of vegetables, herbs and roses. And the Biblical Garden features plants named in the Bible.

Other highlights

Cypress Gardens is called the "Water Ski Capital of the World," and no wonder. The shows are spectacular. And no trip is complete without a visit to the Island in the Sky®. The revolving platform offers a majestic view from 153 feet above the park.

The facts

P.O. Box 1
Cypress Gardens, FL 33884
(863) 324-2111 or (800) 282-2123

Admission: *$31.95 adults, $27.15 ages 55 and older, $14.95 ages 6-17.*

Hours: *Open daily from 9:30 a.m. to 5 p.m. Hours extended during special seasons. Call for information.*

www.cypressgardens.com

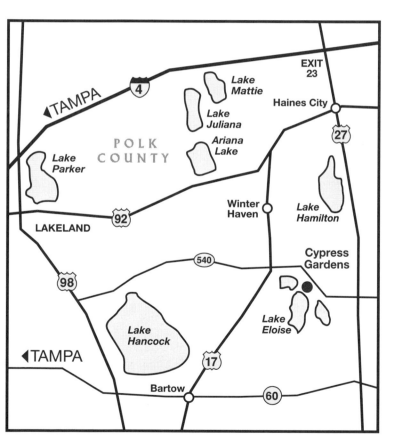

Directions
From Interstate 4, take Exit 23 (U.S. 27) south about 20 miles to State Road 540. Turn right on S.R. 540 and drive about four miles to Cypress Gardens.

"If a picture is worth a thousand words, you'll need a few dictionaries for this place."

▼
17

International Sport Aviation Museum

A.K.A. the Sun 'n Fun Museum

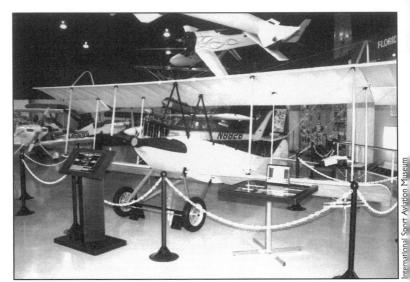

Planes of all shapes, sizes and designs fill the International Sport Aviation Museum.

The trip

Lakeland's annual Sun 'n Fun fly-in is the perfect week for aviation fans. The other 51 weeks of the year, things are quieter here. But don't let that fool you. This museum offers plenty of aviation action.

What to see

This is a perfect place for aviation enthusiasts. Everywhere you turn, an airplane awaits. You can explore the homemade planes, ultralights, antique and classic planes and all types of aircraft engines. And the exhibit of military planes and memorabilia is fascinating.

Other highlights

You don't need to be a pilot to enjoy this museum. Special exhibits cater to all kinds of interests. Check out the collection of Charles Lindbergh memorabilia, the Howard Hughes show at the RKO and uniforms and mementos from the now-defunct National Airlines.

The facts

4175 Medulla Road
Lakeland, FL 33811
(863) 644-0741

Admission: *$4 adults, $2 ages 12 and younger.*

Hours: *Open Monday through Friday 9 a.m. to 5 p.m., Saturday 10 a.m. to 4 p.m., Sunday noon to 4 p.m. Closed on major holidays.*

www.airmuseum.org

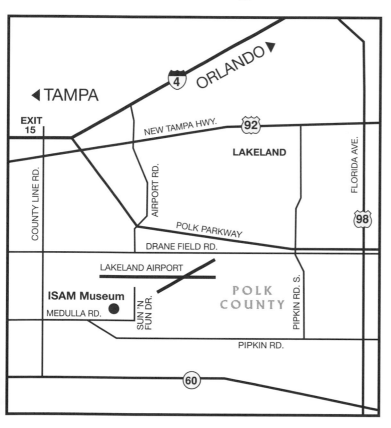

"New expansion projects make this place bigger and better by the day!"

Directions

From Interstate 4, take Exit 15 (County Line Road) south to the third traffic light, which is Medulla Road. Turn left on Medulla and follow it to the museum. The museum is on the southwest corner of Lakeland Linder Regional Airport.

Spook Hill

What Comes Down Goes Up?

Cars appear to go uphill rather than down at Spook Hill. Try it for yourself.

The trip

They call it the mystery of Spook Hill. Don't ask me to explain it. All I know is that cars roll uphill here. This is an inexpensive (make that free) trip for the entire family at a place that would make Newton think twice about his law of gravity.

What to see

The legend says that long ago an Indian chief fought with an alligator. The fight was ferocious. Day after day after day the two battled. Finally the chief vanquished the gator. Some say the evil spirit of the alligator is behind the Spook Hill mischief. Others say the chief is protecting the city from the evil spirit of the alligator, and Spook Hill is the result. Either way, cars still roll up the hill.

To try it, put your car in neutral at North Wales Drive at North Avenue. Release the brake and away you go. You'll have to drive it to believe it. But don't let it drive you mad!

Other highlights

Bok Tower Gardens, another **One Tank** destination, is nearby. You might want to visit both places the same day.

The facts

Lake Wales
Chamber of Commerce
340 W. Central Ave.
Lake Wales, FL 33853
(863) 676-3445

Admission: *Free*

Hours: *Always open.*

www.lakewaleschamber.com

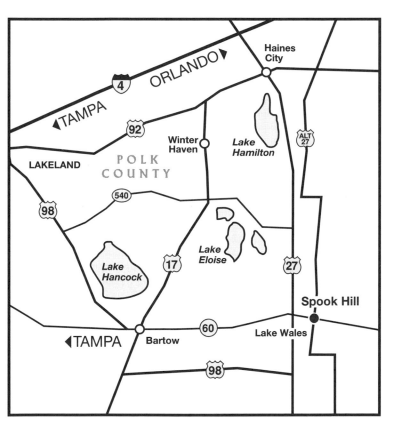

Directions

Head east on State Road 60 to Lake Wales. Turn left at First Street (the first light) and follow it until it ends at North Avenue. Turn right on North Avenue and follow it until it ends on Wales Drive. Spook Hill is on Wales Drive.

"Give it a try – if you dare..."

Daytime Ybor City

Afternoon Delight!

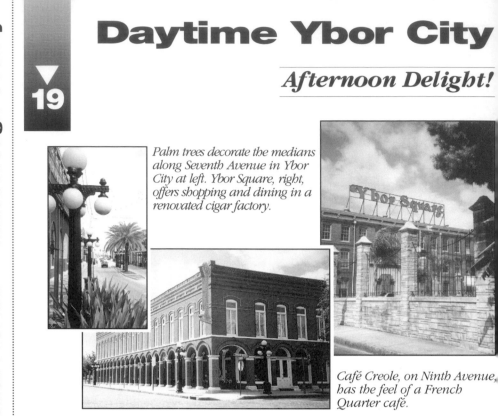

Palm trees decorate the medians along Seventh Avenue in Ybor City at left. Ybor Square, right, offers shopping and dining in a renovated cigar factory.

Café Creole, on Ninth Avenue, has the feel of a French Quarter café.

The trip

Mention Ybor City and some people think of the nightlife, calling it the Tampa Bay area's answer to Bourbon Street. But there's another Ybor City, and you can find it when the sun is out.

What to see

Famed Seventh Avenue offers all kinds of shopping, from specialty gift shops and home decorating, to La Tropicana, an authentic Cuban coffee shop. If you're hungry, try The Columbia Restaurant, which is run by the Gonzmart family. It's the largest and oldest Spanish restaurant in the U.S., and its flamenco show is one of the best in the country. There's also the Silver Ring Café, which is famous for its Cuban sandwich. Or visit Frankie's Patio, a huge casual restaurant with good food.

Tired of the usual museum stop? Take a free tour of the Ybor City Brewing Company. Make sure you also stop by Ybor Square.

Other highlights

Ybor City was once the cigar capital of the world. Today you can still see cigar rollers at work. Even if you don't smoke, you'll enjoy their living history lesson. And the Ybor City State Museum gives you a glimpse of Ybor's cigar industry in its heyday.

The facts

Ybor City Chamber of Commerce
1800 E. Ninth Ave.
Tampa, FL 33605
(813) 248-3712 or
(877) 9 FIESTA (934-3782)

Admission: *Free*

Hours: *Open any day, but call first for hours of the museum and brewing company. Restaurant and shop hours vary.*

www.ybor.org

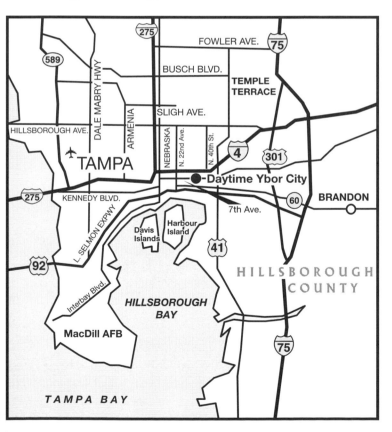

Directions

From Interstate 4, take Exit 1 (21st Street) south to Seventh Avenue, the heart of Ybor City.

"Take the kids on a Sunday afternoon. Or just you and that special someone."

Hillsborough River State Park

A Camper's Delight

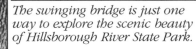

The swinging bridge is just one way to explore the scenic beauty of Hillsborough River State Park.

The trip

On my visit here I learned that the Hillsborough River is named for Wills Hill (1718-93), the Earl of Hillsborough. Set on 2,994 acres, this is one of Florida's oldest parks and, to me, one of the most breathtaking.

What to see

Whether in an R.V. or in a tent, the camping is great. You'll feel like you're in the woods, but with bathrooms and hot showers close by. Hey, I never said I was Daniel Boone! Keep an eye out for the many raccoons and the occasional armadillo.

Other highlights

Rent a canoe and paddle up and down the river. You'll see turtles, all sorts of birds and perhaps an alligator or two. Hike one of the many trails, go fishing or take the plunge in the enormous half-acre swimming pool.

The facts

15402 U.S. 301 N.
Thonotosassa, FL 33592
(813) 987-6771

Admission: *Daily admission is $3.25 per vehicle, swimming is $1 per person. Call for camping rates.*

Hours: *Open daily 8 a.m. to sundown. Open to 10 p.m. Fridays and Saturdays for arriving campers.*

www.dep.state.fl.us/parks

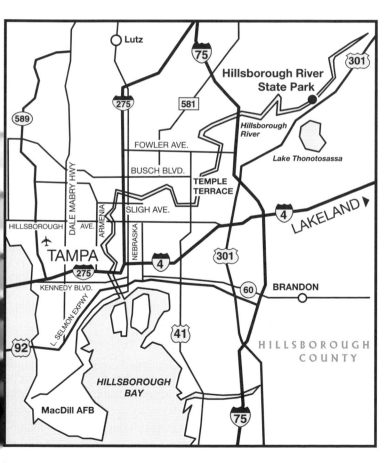

Directions

From Interstate 4, exit on U.S. 301 and head north. The park is 14 miles down the road on the left.

"This is a great place to rough it. For me, that means an R.V. with a black-and-white TV."

▼
21

Lowry Park Zoo

This Place is a Real Zoo!

Red pandas are part of the International Species Survival Program, designed to preserve these endangered animals.

Visitors can observe West Indian manatees in the observation pools at the Florida Manatee and Aquatic Center.

The trip

If you haven't been to the zoo in a while, or ever, stop by. Every visit to this special place is an adventure. The zoo has a wonderful commitment to threatened and endangered species that shows in all of its programs.

What to see

The list of things to do and enjoy and learn is endless. Don't miss the Florida Manatee and Aquatic Center. You'll get a close-up look at Florida's beloved sea mammals. And check out the Egyptian fruit bats. No blood sucking here; they won't attack. They just like to hang around. And on one visit, I got to spend some quality time with Bud. He's a sloth bear and a pretty remarkable creature.

Other highlights

The wildlife shows are spectacular. Here's your chance to get personal with owls and eagles, lizards and frogs. And then there are the fountains. Originally they were designed for show. But the kids had other ideas. Now, jumping in and around the water is part of the zoo tradition.

The facts

7530 North Blvd.
Tampa, FL 33604
(813) 935-8552
(813) 932-0245 (Information Line)

Admission: *$8.50 ages 12-49, $7.50 ages 50 and older,*
$4.95 ages 3-11, 2 and younger are free.

Hours: *Open daily 9:30 a.m. to 5 p.m.*
Closed Thanksgiving and Christmas.

www.lowryparkzoo.com

Directions

From Interstate 275 in Tampa, take the Sligh Avenue exit west and follow the signs to North Boulevard. The zoo is at the corner of Sligh and North Boulevard.

"This place brings out the animal... lots of them."

▼ 22

The Florida Aquarium

Life Down Under

The 152,000-square-foot aquarium tells the story of water in Florida.

The trip

Since March 1995, the aquarium has been telling the story of water and its inhabitants — from wetlands to coral reefs, bays to beaches.

What to see

Discover the variety of sea life in Florida. The Bays & Beaches Gallery features sharks, sea horses and stingrays. Be sure to see the baby jewfish (a type of grouper). The little cutie is only 250 pounds! He will grow to 800 pounds. That's some catch!

Stop by "Dragons Down Under," an amazing display of unique Australian sea dragons — rare and unusual aquatic creatures that are part sea horse and part seaweed.

See what Florida's streams, marshes and rivers have to offer. Here's your chance to meet some otters, egrets and alligators. If you'd rather keep your distance from the gators, climb to the top of the Wetlands Lookout.

Other highlights

Observe more than 1,500 residents of the coral reef through the panoramic window. And stop by the touch pool for your chance to pet live sharks and rays.

The facts

701 Channelside Drive
Tampa, FL 33602
(813) 273-4000

Admission: *$11.95 adults, $10.95 ages 50 and older, $6.95 ages 3-12, free for children younger than 3.*

Hours: *Open daily 9:30 a.m. to 5 p.m. Closed Thanksgiving and Christmas.*

www.flaquarium.org

Directions

From Interstate 275, take Exit 25 (Downtown East and Scott Street) or Exit 26 (Downtown East and Jefferson) and follow the directional signs to the aquarium. From Interstate 4, take Exit 1 (Downtown East) and drive to the second light. Turn left and then right on Palm Avenue. From there, follow the directional signs to the aquarium.

"It gets better on every visit."

Bill Jackson
Shop for Adventure

The Only One of its Kind

From camping to kayaking and beyond, Bill Jackson offers equipment for many outdoor adventures.

The trip

Just a stone's throw from the very busy U.S. 19 in Pinellas Park, tucked away on five acres, is Bill Jackson's — Bill Jackson Shop for Adventure, to be exact, and the adventure is yours for the choosing. For more than half a century, a lot of folks have made this their destination for fun.

What to see

Want to learn to scuba dive? Learn in the 10-foot-deep indoor pool. Skiing? Hit the indoor slopes. There are almost 25,000 square feet of sporting equipment.

Don't worry if you have questions. "Mr. J" insists that the person who helps you is very active in that sport or activity.

Other highlights

Kayaks and canoes come in all shapes, sizes and colors. If you're more interested in fly fishing or archery, they've got just the thing.

The facts

9501 U.S. 19 N.
Pinellas Park, FL 33782
(727) 576-4169

Admission: *Free*

Hours: *Open Monday through Friday 10 a.m. to 9 p.m.,*
Saturday 9:30 a.m. to 6 p.m., Sunday 11 a.m. to 5 p.m.
Closed on major holidays.

www.billjacksons.com

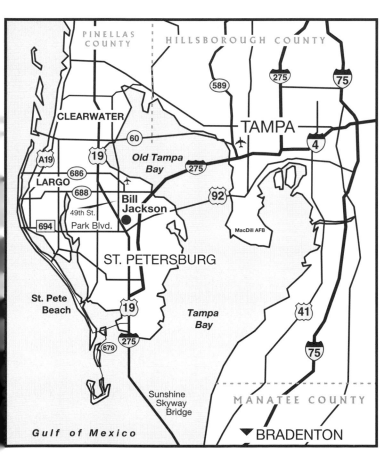

"Plan to spend at least an hour here. The people really know what they're talking about. Imagine that!"

Directions

Bill Jackson's is on U.S. 19 in Pinellas County, one and a half miles north of Park Boulevard and just south of 49th Street.

Boyd Hill
Nature Park

Best Bet for a Buck

Visitors can explore the natural beauty of this park strolling along the miles of trails and boardwalks.

The trip

They call this place "St. Petersburg's Precious Wonder." Set on 245 acres, it's amazing more people don't know about it. Spend just a few minutes here and that "peaceful feeling" will embrace you.

What to see

This unspoiled setting offers more than three miles of trails and boardwalks. You'll see alligators, herons, gopher tortoises and more among the hardwood hammocks, sand pine scrub, pine flatwoods and willow marsh. Or just close your eyes and listen to the crickets, cicadas, woodpeckers and bees. Now that's my kind of noise!

Other highlights

Be sure to see the work of metal sculptor Paul Eppling. At Wax Myrtle Pond you'll find two adventurous armadillos. And two dragon-like creatures guard the park. "Narcissus" lurks at the edge of the pond near the picnic area. "Tree Dragon" or "Forest Mentor" perches on a limb at the rear entrance of the nature center. Bring your camera, your bicycle, if you like, and the hot dogs! There's a picnic area with grills and sheltered tables.

The facts

1101 Country Club Way South St. Petersburg, FL 33705 (727) 893-7326

Admission: *$1 adults, 50 cents ages 3-17, free for children younger than 3.*

Hours: *Open daily 9 a.m. to 5 p.m. During daylight savings time, open until 8 p.m. Tuesday and Thursday. Closed Thanksgiving and Christmas.*

www.stpete.org/nature.htm

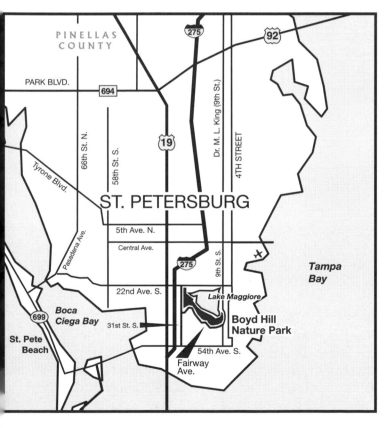

"Fresh air, wildlife, historical architecture and a peaceful oasis in the middle of busy St. Petersburg."

Directions

From Interstate 275, take exit 4 (54th Avenue South) east to Dr. M.L. King Street South (Ninth Street). Turn left and go four blocks to Country Club Way South. Turn left. Boyd Hill Nature Park is on the right.

Captain Memo's
Pirate Cruise

Go Yo-Ho!

Pirates of all ages will enjoy a cruise aboard the Pirate's Ransom.

The trip

Think pirates live only in history books? We found one pirate ship, the "Pirate's Ransom," cleverly hidden away at the Clearwater Beach Marina. I've never met such fun-loving brigands. If you're looking for friendly pirate pleasures, this is the place.

What to see

To join a pirate cruise, you need to get into character. Captain Memo's crew will get you fitted for hats and eye patches. Then it's time to sail the Gulf in search of pirate adventure. There are treasure hunts and pirate stories, games and songs, plus the occasional cannon fire.

Other highlights

The spirited crew will help keep you in the mood for adventure on your two-hour cruise. They'll also help you find dolphins that can be plentiful in the warm Gulf waters. In addition to the daytime cruises, Captain Memo offers champagne cruises, private charters, bay cruises and wedding services.

The facts

25 Causeway Blvd., Clearwater Marina, No. 3 Clearwater, FL 33767 (727) 446-2587

Admission: *Call for rates for various cruises.*
Hours: *Daytime cruises depart at 10 a.m. and 2 p.m. year-round. Additional daily cruises are available from February through September. Call for departures for sunset champagne cruises or special events.*

www.pirateflorida.com

Gulf
Of
Mexico

Mandalay Ave.

Clearwater Harbor

Venetian Point

Sunset Pt. Rd.

Captain Memo's Pirate Cruise

MEMORIAL CSWY

MYRTLE ST.

245

60

DREW ST.

CLEVELAND ST.

COURT ST.

Clearwater Pass

Sand Key

183

CLEARWATER

Harrison

DRUID ROAD

Directions

Take the Courtney Campbell Parkway west to Clearwater. Follow Gulf-to-Bay Boulevard (State Road 60) west across Memorial Causeway to Clearwater Beach. At the end of S.R. 60, turn left onto Mandalay Avenue. Captain Memo's Pirate Cruise is at the Clearwater Marina, just south of the causeway.

"This cruise is non-stop fun!"

Clearwater Marine Aquarium

A Great Stop on the Way to the Beach

Trainer Coni Romano feeds Sunset Sam in the dolphin pool. The pool is a safehouse for dolphins who cannot survive in the wild.

The trip

No doubt many of us have quickly passed the sign. The Clearwater Aquarium sits right off the causeway to Clearwater Beach. In the last 2. years, it's been known as Sea-O-Rama, the Clearwater Marine Scienc Center, even the Florida Marine Aquarium.

What to see

The Clearwater Marine Aquarium is dedicated to the rescue, rehabilitatio and release of sick and injured marine animals. Here you will see a variet of animals that have been rescued.

The real star of the show is Sunset Sam, one of the first dolphins to surviv beaching when he was rescued back in 1984. Back then, he weighed abou 220 pounds. Now he's almost 500 pounds and a real crowd-please Despite a bad eye, he's quite an artist — painting pictures with a speci brush. You can even take home a sample of his artwork!

Other highlights

Ever pet a stingray? Here you can, in a special petting tank. And make sur you visit Mo, a 360-pound turtle named after the battleship U.S.S. Missour He's at least 34 years old — the oldest sea turtle living in captivity.

The facts

249 Windward Passage
Clearwater, FL 33767
(727) 441-1790 or (888) 239-9414

Admission: *$6.75 adults, $4.25 ages 3-11, free for children younger than 3.*

Hours: *Open Monday through Friday 9 a.m. to 5 p.m., Saturday 9 a.m. to 4 p.m., Sunday 11 a.m. to 4 p.m. Closed on major holidays.*

www.cmaquarium.org

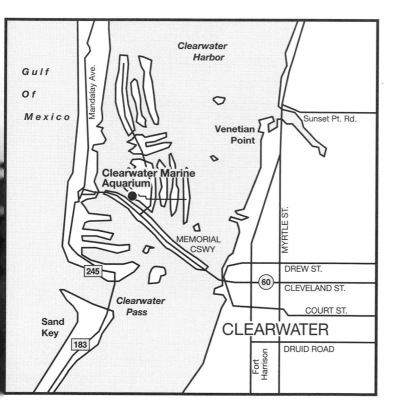

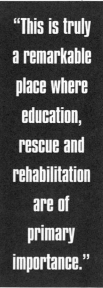

"This is truly a remarkable place where education, rescue and rehabilitation are of primary importance."

Directions

Take State Road 60 in Pinellas County (Gulf-to-Bay Boulevard) west to Memorial Causeway. Follow the causeway until the light at Island Way. Turn right at the light and then left at the single flashing light, which is Windward Passage. The aquarium is on the left.

Fort De Soto Park

A Bay Area Jewel

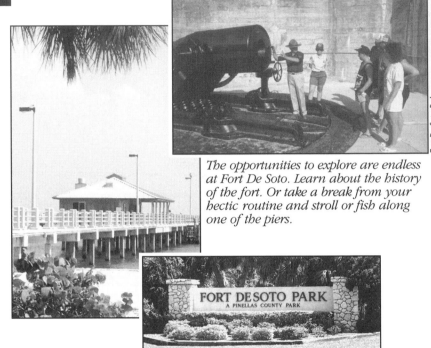

The opportunities to explore are endless at Fort De Soto. Learn about the history of the fort. Or take a break from your hectic routine and stroll or fish along one of the piers.

FORT DE SOTO PARK
A PINELLAS COUNTY PARK

The trip

They call it Pinellas County's most diversified park. Set on five keys, the park includes 900 acres with protected plants and wildlife, miles of beach and fishing piers. Throw in a history lesson at the fort, and there's something for everyone here.

What to see

To start, there's Fort De Soto. The first construction began in 1898 and it was used as a military post until 1923. When you explore the layout of the fort, and its guns, you can't help but learn a little history. Make sure you take the stairs to the top of the fort. The view of the Gulf water and beaches is spectacular.

Other highlights

The 1,000-foot Gulf Pier and 500-foot Bay Pier are wonders for those who fish. And 235 campsites are available for the adventurous. The four-mile recreation trail is perfect for keeping in shape. Finish with a cool drink at the snack bar, and it doesn't get any better than this.

The facts

3500 Pinellas Bayway S.
Tierra Verde, FL 33715
(727) 866-2484 *(Park Patrol and Administration)*
(727) 582-2267 *(Camp Office)*

Admission: *Daily admission to the park is free,*
although there's a toll before you get to the park.
Call for campsite information and rates.
Reservations must be made in person.

Hours: *The park is open daily from sunrise to*
30 minutes after sunset. The camp office is open daily
from 8 a.m. to 9 p.m.

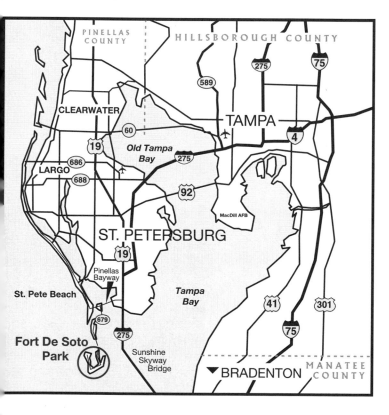

Directions

From Interstate 275, take Exit 4 (Pinellas Bayway) west to the stop light at the Isla Del Sol golf course. Turn left at the light onto State Road 679, which will lead you directly to the park.

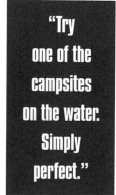

"Try one of the campsites on the water. Simply perfect."

Gulfport Gallery Walk

A Wonderful Little Secret

Visitors stroll and shop through the Gulfport Art Village the first Friday night of every month.

The trip

Only 10 minutes from the Gulf beaches and 15 minutes from downtown St. Petersburg is the quaint and cozy setting of Gulfport. Every month they burn the midnight oil so you can stroll among the displays of works by local artists.

What to see

On the first Friday night of the month and third Saturday night, artists in the Gulfport Art Village display their works for one and all to see. Like paintings? There are plenty of styles to choose from. How about glass work? Here is the kind of stuff that will fire you up and blow you away. You'll also see hand-thrown pottery, handmade jewelry and fine photography.

Other highlights

As you stroll among the booths and shops, enjoy the live entertainment of local musicians. Most shops serve free refreshments, such as wine, cheese and crackers. And when you get tired of walking you can catch a free ride on the city trolley.

The facts

Joann D'Ambra, Events Coordinator
2824 Beach Blvd. S.
Gulfport, FL 33707
(727) 321-7741

Admission: *Free*

Hours: *The Gallery Walk is from 6-10 p.m. on the first Friday evening of the month. The Saturday Stroll is from 6-10 p.m. on the third Saturday of the month.*

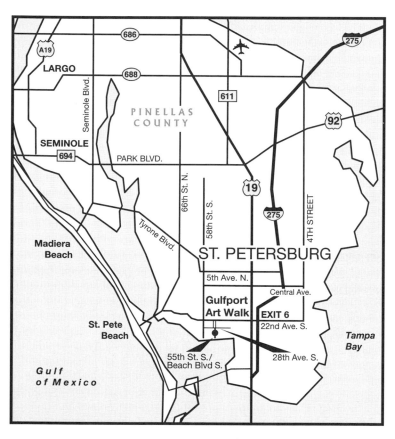

Directions

From Interstate 275, take Exit 6 and head west on 22nd Avenue South. Drive about two miles to Beach Boulevard South (55th Street South) and turn left. The Gulfport Art Village is south of 28th Avenue South on Beach Boulevard (55th Street) in Historic Gulfport.

"The Friday-night walk is a perfect way to kick off the weekend!"

Haslam's Book Store

Simply a Treasure

Haslam's is a local treasure, with a broad range of books to suit any reader's tastes.

The trip

Haslam's calls itself "Florida's greatest rainy-day attraction!" But it certainly doesn't have to be a rainy day to stop by and browse among the 300,000 books.

What to see

Haslam's is the largest independently owned bookstore in the Southeast. Ray and Suzanne Hinst now manage the store for owner Elizabeth Haslam. For 65 years the store has offered new and used books that cater to all kinds of interests — a huge selection of fiction, nonfiction and children's books. Even if you're not sure what you're looking for, stroll among the rows and rows of books. Something's sure to catch your eye.

Other highlights

Haslam's even has its resident ghost, and a literary ghost at that. Jack Kerouac lived in St. Petersburg for a while and would come to Haslam's to rearrange his books so they would sell better. Now, even though he's dead, some believe his ghost is still doing it.

After your visit here, stop by other attractions in lovely downtown St. Petersburg, including The Pier, the Museum of Fine Arts and the Salvador Dali Museum.

The facts

2025 Central Ave.
St. Petersburg, FL 33713
(727) 822-8616

Admission: Free

Hours: Open Monday through Saturday 10 a.m. to 6:30 p.m., Sunday from 12:30 p.m. to 5:30 p.m.

www.haslams.com

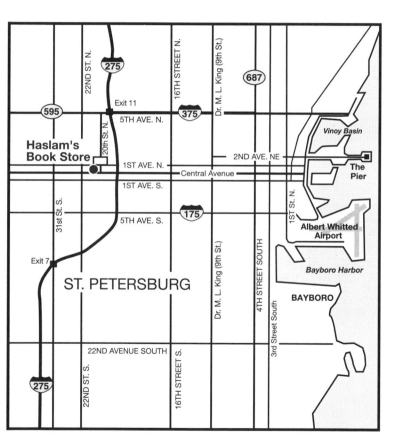

"This is a fine place to pull up a piece of floor and enjoy a good book."

Directions

Driving south on Interstate 275, take Exit 11 to 20th Street. Head south on 20th Street and turn right on Central Avenue. Driving north on I-275, take Exit 7 and turn left on 31st Street. Go seven blocks and turn right on Central Avenue.

Heritage Village

A Blast from the Past

Your walk through history at Heritage Village will include a stop by Heritage Mercantile and the House of Seven Gables, a 13-room Victorian house.

Heritage Village

The trip

Nestled among the pine and palmetto in Largo sits a slice of Florida's past. Explore history at Heritage Village, a collection of more than 20 buildings that serve as a remarkable reminder of the state's rich background.

What to see

You can start with the McMullen-Coachman Loghouse. Built in the 1850s, this house is the oldest existing structure in Pinellas County. And it still rocks. Sit a spell in one of the rocking chairs on the front porch and let history speak to you. Or begin at the Heritage Mercantile store. Not only is the store stocked with goods, there's also a garage and a barbershop full of the stuff of memories.

Other highlights

Among the buildings and museum, you'll be sure to find something that will capture the imagination of every member of your family. There's the House of Seven Gables, a Victorian home; the Harris School, a reproduction of a 1912 one-room schoolhouse; the La France Fire Engine, the first modern fire engine used in Belleair; and the Sulphur Springs Depot and Caboose, a wonderful railroad museum.

The facts

11909 125th St. N.
Largo, FL 33774
(727) 582-2123

Admission: *Free, but donations accepted.*

Hours: *Open Tuesday through Saturday 10 a.m. to 4 p.m., Sunday 1-4 p.m. Closed Mondays and major holidays.*

www.co.pinellas.fl.us/bcc/heritag.htm

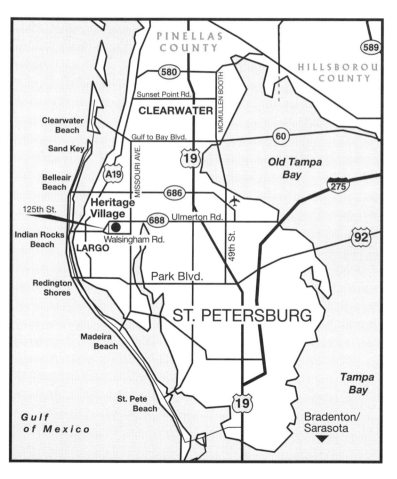

"What a nice surprise to find this place."

Directions

From Interstate 275 or U.S. 19, take the Ulmerton Road (S.R. 688) exit west to 125th Street. Turn left. Heritage Village is on the left.

Museum of Fine Arts

Up Close with the Masters

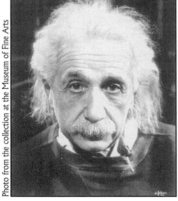

Photo from the collection at the Museum of Fine Arts

"Albert Einstein," by Philippe Halsman, is part of the collection among the 20 galleries at the Museum of Fine Arts.

The trip

You'll find a treasure, make that treasures, beautifully tucked away in downtown St. Petersburg. The Museum of Fine Arts, opened in 1965, is considered one of the finest museums in the Southeast.

What to see

Here I learned that the French artist Pierre Auguste Renoir is called "the painter of the joy of living." In his works on display here, you can see why. Other French artists in the collection include Claude Monet, Paul Cézanne and Auguste Rodin. You'll also see American works, including the brilliant "Poppy," by Georgia O'Keefe.

Other highlights

The building itself is worth a trip, with its beautiful design and exquisite gardens. Stroll through the Sculpture Gardens for a unique experience.

The facts

255 Beach Drive N.E.
St. Petersburg, FL 33701
(727) 896-2667

Admission: *$6 adults, $5 ages 65 and older, $4 for groups of 10 or more, $2 children 7 and older, free for children 6 and younger. Free on Sundays.*

Hours: *Open Tuesday through Saturday 10 a.m. to 5 p.m., Sunday 1-5 p.m. Open the third Thursday of each month until 9 p.m., except summer. Closed every Monday. Closed Christmas and New Year's Day.*

www.fine-arts.org

275

5th Ave. N.
4th Ave. N.

Beach Dr. NE
Bayshore
Vinoy Basin

611

Museum of Fine Arts ●

2ND AVE. NE
1ST AVE. N.
Central Avenue
1ST AVE. S.

92

1ST St. N.

The Pier

19

5th Ave. S.

58th St. S.

275

4TH STREET

Albert Whitted Municipal Airport

ST. PETERSBURG

375

5th Ave. N.
Central Avenue

See inset

Bayboro Harbor

4TH STREET SOUTH

22nd Ave. S.

Tampa Bay

BAYBORO

Tampa Bay

22ND AVENUE SOUTH

Directions

From Interstate 275, exit left onto Interstate 375 east. Take exit 2 (Fourth Avenue North) and follow Fourth until it ends at Beach Drive. Follow Beach Drive south to the museum.

"Whether you're an art lover or just curious, a memorable experience awaits."

Pass-A-Grille

A Resort Feel

The captivating beach and warm Gulf waters on Pass-A-Grille beckon to visitors. And after a day of sun and surf, stop by the Hurricane Seafood Restaurant.

The trip

At the tip of Pinellas County, you'll find a superb seaside destination. And there's no extra charge for the sun, surf, sand and shells.

What to see

History books will tell you Pass-A-Grille was the first established town on the barrier islands of Florida's west coast. But it's also a relaxing place for a day, a week or forever on the beach. This is the perfect spot to dip your toes in the warm Gulf water and stay awhile.

Parking is easier to find here than at most area beaches. But keep those quarters handy. Tickets happen.

Other highlights

Evander Preston's elegant jewelry shop, with exquisite handcrafted gold jewelry, offers much for the discriminating shopper. And beachside concessions offer up gastronomic delights to enjoy while watching the sunset. Visit the Seaside Grill for an early morning breakfast of fresh fruit by the Gulf. The Hurricane Seafood Restaurant, on the Gulf side, is known for its fresh, just-out-of-the-water grouper sandwich.

The facts

Gulf Beaches Chamber of Commerce
St. Pete Beach Office
6990 Gulf Blvd.
St. Pete Beach, FL 33706
(727) 360-6957 or (800) 944-1847

Admission: *Free*

Hours: *The beach is always open. Store and restaurant hours vary.*

www.gulfbeaches-tampabay.com

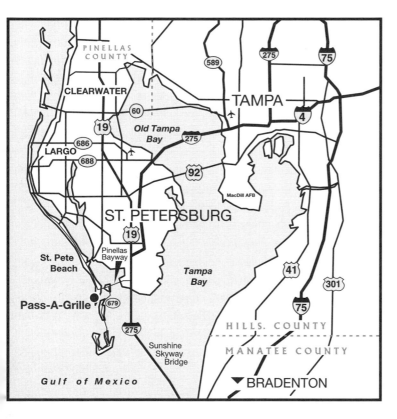

Directions

From Interstate 275, take the St. Pete Beach exit (Pinellas Bayway) west until the bayway stops at the Don CeSar hotel. Turn left onto Gulf Boulevard and follow it to the end, then turn right to the beach.

"One of Pinellas County's most coveted beach spots."

Salvador Dali Museum

Hello, Dali!

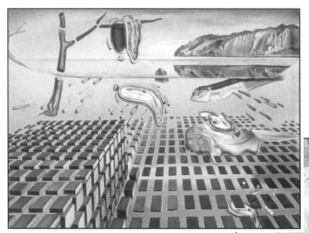

The Disintegration of the Persistence of Memory, *above, and the* Hallucinogenic Toreador, *left, are two of the bewildering and beautiful paintings by surrealist Salvador Dali on display at the museum.*

From the collection at the Salvador Dali Museum

The trip

Set alongside St. Petersburg's beautiful Bayboro Harbor is a local treasure. Inside is the world's most comprehensive collection of works by one of the leaders of the Surrealist art movement in the 20th century, Salvador Dali.

What to see

For the true art lover, or just for the curious, the museum is entertaining as well as educational. In addition to those surreal paintings (does anybody really know what time it is in the melting clock picture?), you'll see dazzling sculptures, holograms and art glass.

Other highlights

Along with the permanent art work on display are special exhibitions of works by other artists. And if you're in the market for some unusual presents, the gift shop can provide a surreal memento or two.

The facts

1000 Third St. S.
St. Petersburg, FL 33701
(727) 823-3767

Admission: *$9 adults, $7 seniors, $5 students with ID (or ages 11 and older), free for ages 10 and younger. Admission is half-price after 5 p.m. on Thursdays.*

Hours: *Open Monday through Saturday 9:30 a.m. to 5:30 p.m. Open Thursdays 9:30 a.m. to 8 p.m. Open Sundays noon to 5:30 p.m. Closed Thanksgiving and Christmas.*

www.daliweb.com

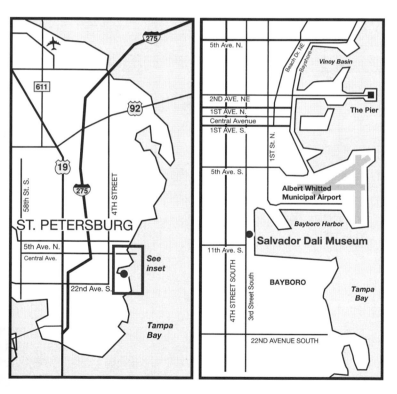

"This place is, to borrow a phrase from the '60s, a real trip!"

Directions

From Interstate 275 in St. Petersburg take Exit 9 and follow I-175 East signs to Fourth Street South. Turn right on Fourth Street. Turn left onto 11th Avenue South, then left to Third Street South.

Sawgrass Lake Park

Mother Nature on Display

Explore the natural beauty of Pinellas County at this scenic park.

The trip

Here in Florida's most densely populated county sits a remarkable 400-acre park of wildlife and natural beauty.

What to see

This is one of Florida's best-kept secrets. Get out your binoculars and marvel at the variety of wildlife. In the short time I was there, I saw alligators, blue heron, osprey, soft-shell turtles, wood stork and a turkey vulture.

Other highlights

More than a mile of scenic boardwalk and an observation tower let you get as close to — or as far from — nature as you want. Bring a picnic! You can sit at one of the shelters and let nature serenade you with the sights and sounds of this lush environment.

The facts

7400 25th St. N.
St. Petersburg, FL 33702
(727) 217-7256

Admission: *Free*

Hours: *Open daily 7 a.m. to dusk.*

www.co.pinellas.fl.us/bcc/park/
sawgrass_lake_park.htm

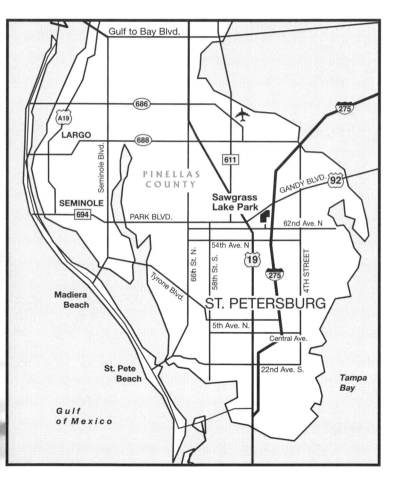

"At every turn, a wonder for the eyes."

Directions

From U.S. 19 in Pinellas County, follow 62nd Avenue North east to 25th Street. Turn left on 25th Street to reach the park.

Tarpon Springs

Bring Your Appetite

Sponge boats and shops are part of the thriving sponge industry in Tarpon Springs.

The trip

Just 30 minutes north of Tampa-St. Petersburg is the enchanted city of Tarpon Springs, a city that is so many things. Greeks began to immigrate to the city in 1906 to work in the sponge industry, and here they have stayed.

What to see

Sponges here come in all shapes and sizes, and shops along the sponge docks offer quite a variety. You can even take a tour on a sponge boat and watch a diver demonstrate sponge harvesting.

If food is something you like, you've come to the right place. The gyros and octopus are mouth-watering. But why save dessert for last? The baklava is to die for.

Other highlights

St. Nicholas Greek Orthodox Church, a monument of love, faith and devotion, is truly magnificent. The church is the center of the Epiphany celebration on Jan. 6 every year. The celebration includes the Greek Cross Ceremony, in which young men dive for a white cross thrown into Spring Bayou. The diver who retrieves the cross is considered to be blessed with good luck for a year. Louis Pappas' restaurant has delicious cuisine and a brilliant waterside view.

The facts

Tarpon Springs
Chamber of Commerce
11 E. Orange St.
Tarpon Springs, FL 34689
(727) 937-6109

Admission: *Free*

Hours: *Restaurant and shop hours vary.*

www.tarponsprings.com

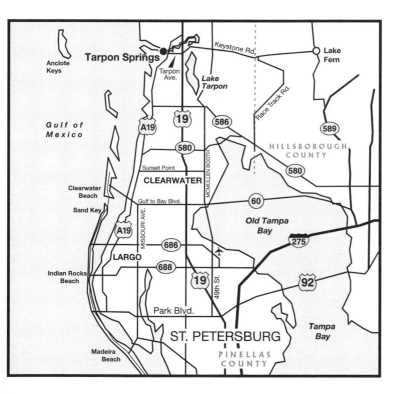

Directions

From U.S. 19, take Tarpon Avenue west to Tarpon Springs. Turn right at Alt. U.S. 19 (Pinellas Avenue) and head north. Turn left at the second stop light (Dodecanese Boulevard). Dodecanese will take you to the sponge dock district. Street parking is limited, but there are lots along Dodecanese.

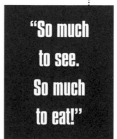

"So much to see. So much to eat!"

Ted Peters
Famous Smoked Fish

Talk About Good Taste!

Smoked mullet and mackerel, smoked to perfection, are the specialties at this landmark restaurant.

The trip

There's something fishy going on around here. For the most part, you can blame Ted Peters. For 50 years his landmark restaurant has been smoking. Literally!

What to see

Ted's smoker keeps busy. You can order any kind of fish you want, as long as it's mullet, mackerel or salmon. They've all been smoked for at least four to five hours in red oak. Add a serving of the restaurant's awesome potato salad, and it's heaven. He and his partners must be doing something right. The indoor-outdoor restaurant has served more than 100,000 pounds of fish a year for years.

Other highlights

The menu's a simple one. They consider an item "new" if it's been on the menu for less than 10 years. And if you're not in the mood for fish, they serve a killer burger.

The facts

1350 Pasadena Ave. S.
St. Petersburg, FL 33707
(727) 381-7931

Admission: Free

Hours: Open Wednesday through Monday 11:30 a.m. to 7:30 p.m. Closed Tuesdays. Closed Thanksgiving and Christmas.

Directions

From Interstate 275 in St. Petersburg, take the Fifth Avenue North exit west to 66th Street. Turn left on 66th Street. It becomes Pasadena Avenue. The restaurant is at 1350 Pasadena Ave. S.

"Take some friends from out of town. They'll thank you forever."

▼
37

The Pier

A St. Petersburg Treasure

Nestled in the waters of Tampa Bay along the St. Petersburg waterfront, The Pier offers a variety of shopping and dining.

The trip

For some, The Pier is a place to drop a fishing line and hope for the best. For others, it's shop 'til you drop. Either way, this upside-down pyramid, all five stories of it, offers plenty to see and do.

What to see

If shopping is your bag, you can fill it here. Clothing and specialty food shops line the first floor of The Pier. If you'd rather be outside, bring your fishing pole and cast your line from the 2,400-foot pier that extends into Tampa Bay.

Other highlights

Would you rather look at fish than catch them? Check out The Pier Aquarium. There are plenty of tropical fish to look at, and some of them even look back. Grab a snack downstairs in the food court. Or head for one of the mouth-watering restaurants The Pier offers, including Spanish cuisine at The Columbia Restaurant and Cha-Cha Coconuts Tropical Bar & Grill.

The facts

800 Second Ave. N.E.
St. Petersburg, FL 33701
(727) 821-6164

Admission: *Free*

Hours: *Open daily at 10 a.m., Sunday 11 a.m. The aquarium is open Monday through Saturday 10 a.m. to 8 p.m., Sunday noon to 6 p.m. Restaurant hours vary.*

www.stpete-pier.com

[Map 1: St. Petersburg area showing 275, 611, 92, 19, 4th Street, 58th St. S., 375, 5th Ave. N., Central Ave., 22nd Ave. S., Tampa Bay, ST. PETERSBURG, See inset]

[Map 2 (inset): 5th Ave. N., 4th Ave. N., 2ND AVE. NE, 1ST AVE. N., Central Avenue, 1ST AVE. S., 5th Ave. S., 1ST St. N., 4TH STREET SOUTH, 22ND AVENUE SOUTH, Beach Dr. NE, Bayshore, Vinoy Basin, The Pier, Albert Whitted Municipal Airport, Bayboro Harbor, BAYBORO, Tampa Bay]

Directions

From Interstate 275, take Exit 10 east and follow Fourth Avenue North to Beach Drive. Turn south to Second Avenue N.E. The Pier is at the east end of Second Avenue.

"A fun destination day or night."

Gamble Plantation State Historic Site

Heaven for History Buffs

38

The mansion at the Gamble Plantation is the only antebellum plantation house surviving in south Florida.

The trip

One of southwest Florida's first settlers built this sugar plantation next to the Manatee River in Ellenton. Today, it's a living history lesson for visitors.

What to see

In the mid-1800s, Major Robert Gamble built one of the most successful sugar plantations in Florida. His mansion reflected his success. It was one of the finest homes on Florida's southwest coast. On your tour of the mansion, you'll see the house furnished in 19th-century style, depicting the lavish scale of the operation.

Even the mansion's construction is a history lesson. Two-foot-wide walls kept residents cool in the summer and offered protection from hurricanes. And a "dogtrot" separated the north section from the main building.

Other highlights

The mansion also played a role in the history of the Civil War. Confederate Secretary of State Judah P. Benjamin hid at the mansion after the fall of the Confederacy in 1865. From here, he escaped to England. Today the mansion marks his famous escape.

The facts

Gamble Plantation State Historic Site
3708 Patten Ave.
Ellenton, FL 34222
(941) 723-4536

Admission: *Admission to the site is free. Visits at the mansion are by tour only. Tour fees are $3 for adults, $1.50 for ages 6-12, free for children younger than 6.*

Hours: *Site is open daily from 8 a.m. to sunset. Call for a tour schedule.*

www.dep.state.fl.us/parks/ gamble plantation/gamble plantation.html

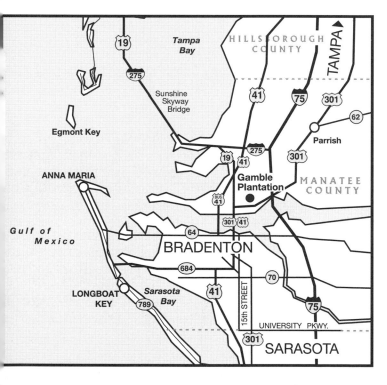

Directions

From Interstate 75, take the U.S. 301 exit west one mile. The entrance is on the right.

"At every turn, a history lesson."

▼
39

Linger Lodge
R.V. Resort & Restaurant

A Little Bit of Everything

Relax on the deck of the Linger Lodge Restaurant, which overlooks the picturesque Braden River.

The trip

Nestled along the beautiful Braden River, I found the perfect place to linger awhile.

What to see

The setting is Old Florida at its best. There are more than 10 acres of peace and quiet at this R.V. resort. You can park your R.V. at one of the waterfront lots or park among the natural beauty of the palm and pine trees. The secluded Braden River flows along the south side and it's a fishing paradise.

You don't need an R.V. to stop by. The unique restaurant has brought people here for years. Do they come for the grilled sandwiches and chicken pot pie? Well, yes. But they also are here to see owner and storyteller Frank Gamsky. Ever hear of Alaskan fur fish or jack-a-lopes? Frank can tell you all about them. Hundreds of creatures — some more unusual than others — are mounted and on display in the restaurant.

Other highlights

The area is rich with wildlife. Frank saved some wild boar babies from a ferocious gator. Now they live across the river from him. There's also a Chinese golden pheasant. It's the most beautiful bird I've ever seen. And on a ride down the river you'll see softshell turtles, native birds and plenty of alligators.

The facts

7205 Linger Lodge Road
Bradenton, FL 34202
(941) 755-2757

Admission: *Call for lot rental rates.*

Office hours: *Open Tuesday through Sunday noon to 6 p.m. Closed Mondays year-round. Closed Tuesdays May 1 to Nov. 1.*

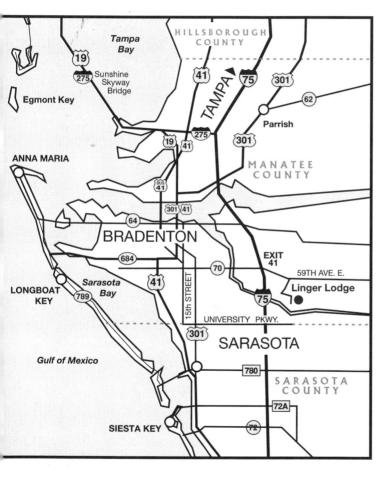

Directions

From Interstate 75, take Exit 41 (S.R. 70) east. Turn right on Braden Run, right on Forrester Drive and then right again onto Oak Hammock. Oak Hammock runs right into Linger Lodge.

"Beauty abounds here. It's a very pleasant way to get away from it all."

South Florida Museum, Bishop Planetarium & Parker Manatee Aquarium

▼ 40

Three for the Price of One

The South Florida Museum is the home of manatees, memorabilia and magnificent stars.

The trip

This place is really three trips in one: the South Florida Museum, th Bishop Planetarium and the Parker Manatee Aquarium. There's so muc to see and do that you'll have quite a day here.

What to see

The 220-seat planetarium is a wonder of planets and stars. On my visit th stars were the Stones — a laser fantasy show set to the music of the Rollin Stones. The South Florida Museum lets you get close to history. Amon the exhibits are artifacts from the Native Americans who first lived her pioneer artifacts and the White House bedroom set of Ulysses S. Grant.

Other highlights

Make sure you meet Snooty at the Parker Manatee Aquarium. He' Manatee County's official manatee mascot. You can't help but fall in lov with him and his manatee playmate, Mo. And don't miss the Discover Place, a hands-on center for kids of all ages and sizes.

The facts

201 10th St. W.
Bradenton, FL 34205
(941) 746-4131

Admission: *$7.50 adults, $6 ages 60 and older,*
$4 ages 5-12, free for preschoolers.

Hours: *Open Tuesday through Saturday 10 a.m. to*
5 p.m., Sunday noon to 5 p.m. Closed Thanksgiving,
Christmas and New Year's Day. Call for a schedule of
manatee and planetarium programs.

www.sfmbp.org

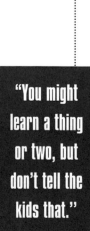

"You might learn a thing or two, but don't tell the kids that."

Directions

From Interstate 75, take Exit 42 (State Road 64). Go west to 10th Street West and then right three blocks to the museum.

Ca' d'Zan, the Ringling Winter Residence

Such Elegance!

▼ 41

John and Mable Ringling's winter residence was designed to evoke the splendor of Venetian Gothic palaces with columns in the courtyard and the sculpture of the Fountain of Oceanus.

The trip

The winter residence of John and Mable Ringling, set on scenic Sarasota Bay, is nothing short of magnificent. Stand on the terrace and soak in the spectacular view of the bay and barrier islands. Once inside, see how the rich and famous used to live. The house was recently featured in the film "Great Expectations" starring Gwyneth Paltrow.

What to see

Called Ca' d'Zan, or "House of John" in Venetian dialect, the house is 200 feet long, with 30 rooms and 14 baths. The home reflects the Ringlings' taste in architecture with its breathtaking style and attention to detail. It took two years to build their monument to Venetian palaces here on Florida's west coast. The house was finished in 1926 and cost about $1.5 million. Inside, explore the Ringlings' collection of furniture and paintings — a glimpse of the good life in the Roaring '20s.

Other highlights

Don't leave without a trip to the rest of the museum complex. More than 500 years of European art are on display in the fabulous museum. Love the circus? See the costumes, posters, props and circus wagons in the Museum of the Circus.

The facts

5401 Bay Shore Road
Sarasota, FL 34243
(941) 359-5700

Admission: *$9 adults, $8 ages 55 and over, free for ages 12 and younger, free for Florida students and teachers with valid ID cards. Admission to the art museum only is free on Saturdays.*

Hours: *Open daily 10 a.m. to 5:30 p.m. Closed New Year's Day, Thanksgiving and Christmas.*

www.ringling.org

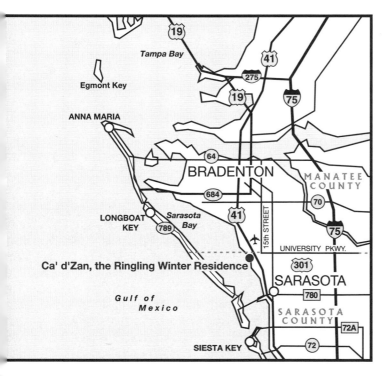

Directions

From Interstate 75, take exit 40 (University Parkway) west to Sarasota until it ends at the museum. The museum is at the intersection of University Parkway and U.S. 41, just south of the Sarasota-Bradenton International Airport.

"This house is a feast for the eyes."

Historic Spanish Point

My Kind of History Lesson

The rooms in the Guptill House, built in 1901 by Frank and Lizzie Webb Guptill, feature exhibits from the period.

The trip

This 30-acre site between Sarasota and Venice offers a fascinating history lesson. Exhibits here take you from prehistoric times to the early 20th century.

What to see

You can start with ancient history. Go inside a midden, or shell mound. These ancient "trash heaps," with tools, bones and other artifacts, are a virtual history book of the lives of native peoples from 2000 B.C. to 1000 A.D.

When you're ready for more modern times, head to the Guptill House. It's just one of a collection of buildings that let you explore pioneer life in Florida from 1867 to 1910. After you walk through the homestead house, visit the pioneer cemetery, chapel and citrus packing house.

Other highlights

From 1910 to 1918, Bertha Matilde Honore' Palmer left her own mark on Spanish Point — magnificent formal lawns and gardens designed around the pioneer dwellings and native remains. If you prefer a little wilderness in its natural state, walk along the nature trails.

The facts

337 N. Tamiami Trail
P.O. Box 846
Osprey, FL 34229
(941) 966-5214

Admission: *$7 adults, $5 senior citizens on Mondays, $3 ages 6-12.*

Hours: *Open Monday through Saturday 9 a.m. to 5 p.m., Sunday noon to 5 p.m. Closed on major holidays. Guided tours are offered daily. Call for tour times.*

www.historicspanishpoint.org

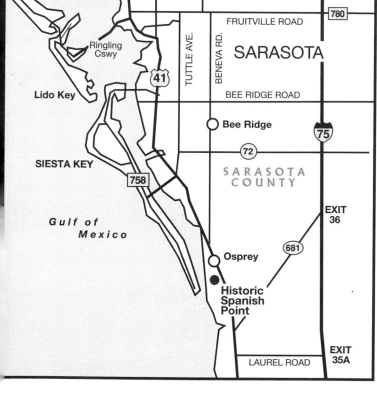

Directions

From Interstate 75, take Exit 36 or 35A west to U.S. 41. Turn right on U.S. 41. The entrance to Historic Spanish Point is on the left.

"5,000 years of history in one place."

Marie Selby Botanical Gardens

A Treat for the Eyes...and Nose

The enchanting Dove or Holy Ghost orchid, above, and Butterfly orchid, left, are among the 6,000 orchids on display.

Theophil Kuczynski

The trip

It's been called "a supernova in the constellation of botanical gardens." The beauty here is inescapable.

What to see

Selby Gardens is a living outdoor and under-glass museum of more than 20,000 plants, each of them more breathtaking than the last. At every turn a photo opportunity awaits. Perhaps this place is best known for it living collection of more than 6,000 orchids. These treasures will steal your heart.

Other highlights

A stop by the butterfly garden is a must. And make sure you see th amazing banyan grove. It's almost as though arms and hands are reachin out to you from the roots and branches. Among the 20 distinct garden are the spectacular bromeliad display, the palm grove and the koi pond with some of the healthiest fish I've ever seen.

The facts

811 S. Palm Ave.
Sarasota, FL 34236
(941) 366-5731

Admission: *$8 adults, $4 children 6-11, free for under 5.*

Hours: *Open daily 10 a.m. to 5 p.m. Closed Christmas.*

www.selby.org

Directions

From Interstate 75, take Exit 39 (Fruitville Road) west to U.S. 41. Follow U.S. 41 south to Palm Avenue.

"One of the most enchanting places you'll ever visit."

Mote Marine Aquarium

A "Must See" in Sarasota

This fish is one of the more than 200 varieties of fish and invertebrates you can see at the aquarium.

The trip

Mote Marine Aquarium has always been a special place. Near St Armands Circle in Sarasota, it displays the treasure of riches the sea holds.

What to see

"Look, touch and explore" is the motto here. A 30-foot touch tank lets you do just that. Ever wondered what stingrays feel like? Here's your chance to find out. More than 20 viewing tanks display eels, turtles starfish and sea plants. Don't miss the 135,000-gallon outdoor shar tank. It's a display with some teeth.

Other highlights

The aquarium is connected to the Mote Marine Laboratory, so you can ge a close-up look at research in progress. You can also visit the Marin Mammal Center, with its sea turtle rehabilitation area and a pair c manatees, Hugh and Buffett, half-brothers that live at the center.

The facts

1600 Ken Thompson Parkway
Sarasota, FL 34236
(941) 388-2451

Admission: *$10 adults, $7 ages 4-17, free for children younger than 4.*

Hours: *Open daily 10 a.m. to 5 p.m.*

www.mote.org

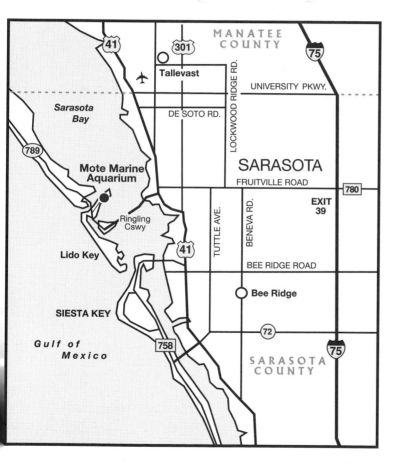

"This place will soothe the savage beast in you and will please kids of all ages."

Directions

From Interstate 75, take Exit 39 (Fruitville Road) west to U.S. 41. Turn south on U.S. 41 to Ringling Causeway, turn right and cross the causeway. Then follow the signs to the aquarium.

St. Armands Circle

A Shopper's Paradise

Stroll through the shops or relax in the restaurants that St. Armands Circle offers.

Sarasota Convention and Visitors Bureau

The trip

It's been called the Rodeo Drive of Florida. St. Armands Circle sits on St. Armands Key. The key was purchased by Charles St. Amand in 1893 for a whopping $21.71. (I guess you could call that a good investment.) But his name was misspelled in land deeds as St. Armands, and that name has stuck to the area ever since.

What to see

More than 100 shops and restaurants — from fine food to fabulous jewels to fashion to fun stuff for Fido — are nestled on St. Armands Circle. When you're done shopping, stroll along the shopping circle and admire the lush tropical landscaping.

Other highlights

Beautiful Lido Beach is a short drive away. After a day of shopping and eating, a sunset stroll is the perfect way to top off your visit.

The facts

St. Armands Circle Association
P.O. Box 6034
Sarasota, FL 34278
(941) 388-1554

Admission: *Free*

Hours: *Store and restaurant hours vary. Most stores are open Monday through Saturday from 9:30 a.m. to 5:30 p.m. Some stores are open evenings and Sundays.*

www.starmandscircle.com

Directions

From Interstate 75, take Sarasota Exit 39 (Fruitville Road) and head west on State Road 780 to St. Armands Key.

Sarasota Bay Explorers

An Outdoor Odyssey

Guided tours are the perfect way to explore marine life.

The trip

A kayak trip with Sarasota Bay Explorers is a three-hour adventure of fun, exercise and education through Sarasota Bay to South Lido Park. Or you can take the scenic pontoon tour, which lasts almost two hours.

What to see

No experience is necessary for this tour. You'll get lessons from a pro. Everyone in our group picked up the art of kayaking pretty quickly, and soon we were headed for the water.

While you're on the water, you'll hear from a biologist about the wildlife in the area. Paddling through the backwater is a perfect way to get an education about flora and fauna and get a little workout at the same time.

Sarasota Bay Explorers also offer sea life encounter tours of Sarasota Bay and Roberts Bay aboard a 40-foot pontoon boat. Or you can design your own charter for up to six people aboard the 24-foot "Miss Explorer," which comes with a captain and a naturalist guide.

The facts

Sarasota Bay Explorers sail from
Mote Marine Aquarium
1600 Ken Thompson Parkway
Sarasota, FL 34236
(941) 388-4200

Admission: *Kayak tours are $50 adults, $40 ages 4-17; sea life encounter tours are $24 for adults, $20 for ages 4-17; charters are $275 for four hours, $375 for six hours.*

Hours: *Kayak tours are on Monday, Wednesday and Friday from 10 a.m. to 1 p.m. Call for times for the daily sea life encounter tours and to make reservations for all the tours.*

isurus.marinelab.sarasota.fl.us /~mkmetz/sarabay.htm

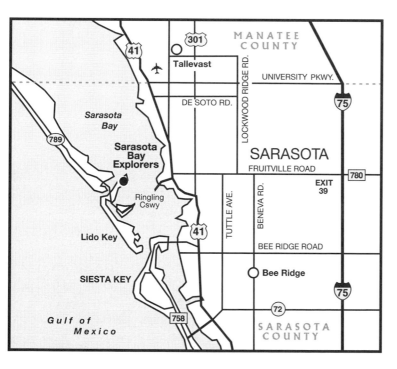

Directions

From Interstate 75, take Exit 39 (Fruitville Road) west to U.S. 41. Turn south on U.S. 41 to Ringling Causeway, turn right and cross the causeway. Then follow the signs to the aquarium.

"This is an experience you'll long remember."

Sarasota
Classic Car Museum

Get Your Motor Running

The Sarasota Classic Car Museum is the perfect stop for the chrome lover. The collection of cars is a tribute to engineering days gone by.

Sarasota Classic Car Museum

The trip

Within walking distance of the Ringling Museum in Sarasota is another amazing collection of a different kind of art — classic cars.

What to see

This car museum flipped me out. There's the 1958 Plymouth featured in the horror classic, "Christine," and possibly the only '57 Chevy ambulance in existence. If you're a fanatic about fins, check out the '59 Cadillac El Dorado. And if you prefer two wheels, there's a rare 1947 Indian Chief motorcycle.

Other highlights

Don't miss the antique game arcade. You'll feel like you were in the Coney Island of the 1950s. And stop by the Great Music Hall to see Thomas Edison's diamond-tip record-needle phonograph. Or check out the collection of player pianos, music boxes and player nickelodeons.

The facts

5500 N. Tamiami Trail
Sarasota, FL 34243
(941) 355-6228

Admission: *$8.50 adults, $7.65 seniors, $5.75 for ages 13-17, $4 for ages 6-12, free for children 5 and younger.*

Hours: *Open daily 9 a.m. to 6 p.m.*

www.sarasotacarmuseum.org

"A party for the eyes and ears."

Directions
From Interstate 75, take Exit 40 (University Parkway) west to Sarasota. The museum is at the intersection of University Parkway and U.S. 41.

▼
48

Sarasota Jungle Gardens

It's a Jungle Out There!

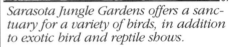

Sarasota Jungle Gardens offers a sanctuary for a variety of birds, in addition to exotic bird and reptile shows.

The trip

Sarasota Jungle Gardens offers you a truly tropical experience. There are plenty of birds to love — well, except for the gull that ate my lunch.

What to see

Snakes alive! This place has plenty of them, including the rare, and beautiful, Florida indigo snake. The daily reptile shows give you a chance to get personal with our scaly neighbors.

Other highlights

This is also a lemur-friendly neighborhood that is home to flamingos, monkeys, leopards and a giant tortoise. Check out those feathered friends in the daily bird shows that feature cockatoos and macaws.

The facts

3701 Bay Shore Road
Sarasota, FL 34234
(941) 355-5305

Admission: *$9 teens and adults,*
$8 ages 62 and older, $5 for ages 3-12.

Hours: *Open daily 9 a.m. to 5 p.m.*
Closed Christmas.

www.sarasotajunglegardens.com

Directions

From Interstate 75, take exit 40 (University Parkway) west to Sarasota until it ends at U.S. 41. Turn left on U.S. 41 and go four blocks to Myrtle Street. Turn right on Myrtle and go two blocks to the gardens.

"This is a picture-taking paradise. Especially the birds!"

Arcadia

Old-Fashioned Friendliness

The Old Opera House sits on Polk Street in downtown Arcadia.

© 1986 Artion Photography

The trip

While a travel book I have calls it "Cowboy Town," the lovely community of Arcadia is much more. One author named it "The Best Small Town in Florida," and a stroll through the charming historic district will prove it.

What to see

Old town Arcadia boasts 20 antique and specialty shops, with plenty of charming collectibles and an abundance of friendly folks. And if you like architecture, the historic district includes some prime examples from the early 1900s. Your day trip should include lunch, of course, and there are plenty of restaurants — from ice cream shops to country cooking — to go around.

Other highlights

Stop by the Oak Ridge Cemetery. Twenty-three Royal Air Force cadets died while training in Florida during World War II. Their remains are here at a special British section of the cemetery where the Union Jack flies daily — young men forever.

The facts

DeSoto County
Chamber of Commerce
16 S. Volusia Ave.
Arcadia, FL 34266
(941) 494-4033

Admission: *Free*

Hours: *Shop and restaurant hours vary.*

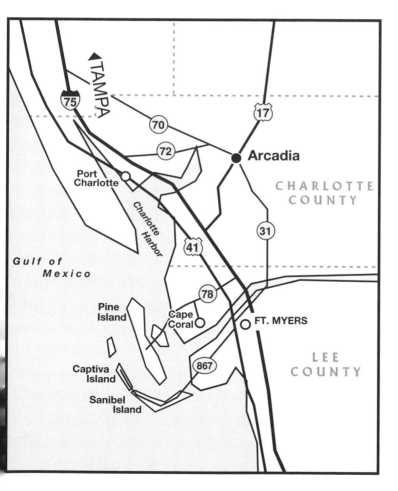

"Arcadia has a homespun charm. You'll be pleasantly surprised and warmly greeted."

Directions

From Interstate 75, exit on State Road 70 and follow it east about 40 miles to historic downtown Arcadia.

Canoe Outpost at Peace River

50

Give Peace a Chance

A canoe trip down the Peace River is the perfect way to restore your peace of mind.

The trip

This is my kind of adventure! It begins with a stop at the Canoe Outpost, a family-run business that was the first canoe outfitter in the state. From there it's a bus ride, canoes in tow, to the place where you start your "downstream" paddle on the Peace River.

What to see

The Peace River has some of the most beautiful canoe trails in the state. The river itself runs from the Green Swamp all the way to the Gulf of Mexico. It's more than 100 miles long, and 63 miles are designated canoe trails.

You can take the half-day trip or stay out overnight along the river. Either way, make sure you take your time and enjoy the scenery. Don't worry about carrying your supplies. The folks at Canoe Outpost will get your gear to the campground on the overnight trips. They'll even provide it for you.

Other highlights

Stop whenever you like along the river to swim, fish, hike or go fossil hunting. This is a great place to explore. And if you have time, visit nearby Arcadia, another **One Tank** destination.

The facts

2816 N.W. County Road 661
Arcadia, FL 34266
(800) 268-0083

Leisure paddle: $25 per canoe for 2 people,
$8 each additional person.
12 and younger free as extra person.

Call for weekday and weekend departure times.

www.canoeoutpost.com

Directions

From Interstate 75, take Exit 41 (State Road 70) east for 39 miles. Turn north on C.R. 661 at Peace River Campground. The Canoe Outpost is on the right behind the campground. Look for the "canoe" mailbox.

"A beautiful river that is well-named."

Captiva Island

Florida's Tahiti

Blind Pass separates the barrier islands, and stunning beaches, of Captiva and Sanibel.

© Lee Island Coast

© Lee Island Coast

The trip

You will love your visit to the barrier island of Captiva. The setting is picturesque and then some. Captiva and its sister island, Sanibel, offer incredible natural beauty.

What to see

Captiva Beach has been called "Florida's Most Romantic and Best Sunset Beach," and it's easy to see why. The sand and surf are glorious. And the shells! This is a shell collector's paradise, no matter the time of year. Sunrise is the best time to find a treasure.

Other highlights

For those who enjoy fishing, it's like dying and going to heaven. Bring your own pole and boat or arrange a charter. And stop by Chapel by the Sea. This tiny chapel, once the one-room schoolhouse on the island, still is the site of worship services from November through April. There's plenty of great shopping, especially at the shops near South Seas Resort and Yacht Harbor.

The facts

Sanibel & Captiva Islands Chamber of Commerce
1159 Causeway Road
Sanibel Island, FL 33957
(941) 472-1080

Admission: *Free, although there is a $3 toll on the causeway. Beach-access parking is 75¢ an hour.*

Hours: *Public park beaches close at dusk. Restaurant, shop and attraction hours vary.*

www.sanibel-captiva.org

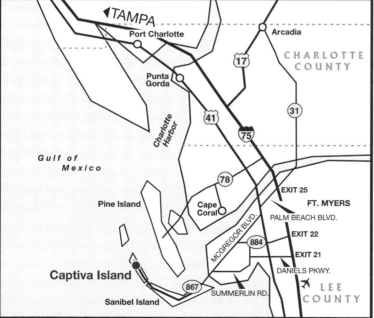

Directions

From Interstate 75, take Exit 21 (Daniels Parkway) west to Summerlin Road. Follow Summerlin Road across the Sanibel Causeway (a $3 toll) to Sanibel Island. At the four-way stop, turn right on Periwinkle Way. Turn right at Tarpon Bay and left on Sanibel-Captiva Road. Drive about eight miles and cross Blind Pass bridge and you're on Captiva Island.

"From the beach, to a book, to a bite of lunch, this is indeed a wondrous place to get away from it all."

▼
52

Edison-Ford Winter Estates

Lee County Luxury

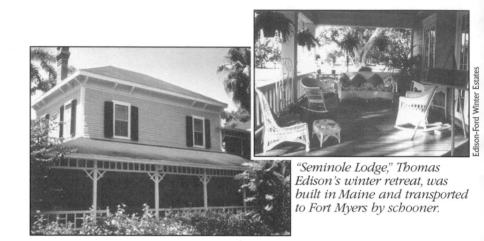

"Seminole Lodge," Thomas Edison's winter retreat, was built in Maine and transported to Fort Myers by schooner.

Edison-Ford Winter Estates

The trip

As the new millennium approaches, pay a visit to the winter home of the person Life magazine named the man of this millennium — inventor Thomas Alva Edison.

What to see

Edison loved this setting along the Caloosahatchee River. He would spend hours fishing off the pier — without any bait on the hook. He was here to think, not catch fish.

He conducted his last major experiments in the laboratory here. Today, the lab looks about the same, with its test tubes and research. His "cat-nap" cot still sits in the lab, ready to be used.

Edison once said, "Of all my inventions, I like the phonograph best." More than 200 are on display in the Edison Museum. You can also see his Model T Ford, a gift from friend Henry Ford. And take a ride on one of four electric launches. They are similar to the one Edison bought in 1903.

Other highlights

Henry Ford came to visit the Edisons in 1915. In 1916 he bought the house next door for his own winter home. Together these two estates display the life and times of two remarkable families.

The facts

2350 McGregor Blvd.
Fort Myers, FL 33901
(941) 334-3614

Admission: *$12 adults January through April, $11 adults May through December, $5.50 ages 6-12, free for children younger than 6.*

Hours: *Open Monday through Saturday 9 a.m. to 4 p.m., Sunday noon to 4 p.m. Closed Thanksgiving and Christmas.*

www.edison-ford-estate.com

"Be sure to spend some time in the gardens. You've never seen anything like it!"

Directions

From Interstate 75, take Exit 22 (Colonial Boulevard) west to U.S. 41. Turn right on U.S. 41 and follow it to Edison Avenue. Turn left on Edison Avenue and follow the signs to the estates.

WEATHER GUIDE

	Fort Myers		Jacksonville		Key West		Miami	
	High/Low	Rainfall	High/Low	Rainfall	High/Low	Rainfall	High/Low	Rainfall
January	74°/53°	1.8"	64°/42°	3.3"	75°/65°	2.0"	75°/59°	2.0"
February	76°/54°	2.2"	67°/44°	3.9"	75°/65°	1.8"	76°/60°	2.1"
March	80°/59°	3.1"	74°/50°	3.7"	79°/69°	1.7"	79°/64°	2.4"
April	85°/62°	1.1"	80°/56°	2.8"	82°/72°	1.8"	83°/68°	3.0"
May	89°/68°	3.9"	85°/63°	3.6"	85°/76°	3.5"	85°/72°	6.2"
June	91°/73°	9.5"	89°/70°	5.7"	88°/79°	5.1"	88°/75°	9.3"
July	91°/75°	8.3"	92°/73°	5.6"	89°/80°	3.6"	89°/77°	5.7"
August	91°/75°	9.7"	91°/72°	7.9"	89°/79°	5.0"	89°/77°	7.6"
September	90°/74°	7.8"	87°/70°	7.1"	88°/79°	5.9"	88°/76°	7.6"
October	86°/69°	2.9"	80°/60°	2.9"	84°/76°	4.4"	85°/72°	5.6"
November	81°/61°	1.6"	73°/50°	2.2"	80°/71°	2.8"	80°/67°	2.7"
December	76°/55°	1.6"	67°/44°	2.7"	76°/67°	2.0"	77°/62°	1.8"

	Orlando		Pensacola		Tampa Bay		Tallahassee	
	High/Low	Rainfall	High/Low	Rainfall	High/Low	Rainfall	High/Low	Rainfall
January	72°/51°	2.3"	60°/41°	4.7"	70°/49°	2.0"	63°/38°	4.8"
February	72°/50°	4.0"	63°/44°	5.4"	71°/51°	3.1"	66°/40°	5.5"
March	78°/56°	3.2"	69°/51°	5.7"	77°/56°	3.0"	73°/47°	6.2"
April	84°/61°	1.3"	76°/58°	3.4"	82°/61°	1.2"	80°/52°	3.7"
May	88°/67°	3.1"	83°/66°	4.2"	87°/67°	3.1"	86°/61°	4.8"
June	91°/72°	7.5"	89°/72°	6.4"	90°/73°	5.5"	91°/68°	6.9"
July	92°/74°	7.2"	90°/74°	7.4"	90°/74°	6.6"	91°/71°	8.8"
August	91°/74°	7.1"	89°/74°	7.3"	90°/74°	4.6"	91°/71°	7.5"
September	89°/73°	6.3"	86°/70°	5.4"	89°/73°	6.0"	88°/68°	5.6"
October	84°/67°	2.9"	79°/60°	4.1"	84°/65°	2.0"	81°/56°	2.9"
November	77°/57°	1.7"	70°/51°	3.5"	78°/57°	1.8"	73°/46°	3.9"
December	73°/52°	2.0"	63°/44°	4.3"	72°/52°	2.2"	66°/41°	5.0"

A Word about the Weather

Hi everybody,

As you make your plans to travel around Florida on your **One Tank Trips**, I thought you would like to know the average high and low temperatures and rainfall. I've prepared the accompanying chart that you can use as a reference. Keep in mind that afternoon rains in the summer are almost a daily occurrence.

Also remember that hurricane season runs from June until the end of November. If you are in an area in which a hurricane is approaching, I urge you to take the warnings seriously. If authorities call for an evacuation, follow their instructions.

For the latest on the weather in the Tampa Bay area, give us a call at **(813) 871-1313**, and then press 1. Enjoy your travels!

Paul Dellegatto
Paul Dellegatto
FOX13 Chief Meteorologist

Sunshine State Sports

Catch the excitement of a Devil Rays game at Tropicana Field in St. Petersburg.

© 1998 Robert Rogers Tampa Bay Devil Rays

© Glenda Jones

© 1999 Tampa Bay Buccaneers

Raymond James Stadium in Tampa is home to the Tampa Bay Buccaneers, the Tampa Bay Mutiny and the USF Bulls.

Watch the Lightning take the ice at the Ice Palace in Tampa.

© 1997 Ice Palace

A Word about Sports

As you look through the following sports attractions list, you can see that our Sunshine State is serious about sports. These aren't just sports spots; these are great family destinations that my family has enjoyed.

Incredibly, as our staff put this list together, I realized I can personally vouch for every venue on this list. In my travels with **FOX13 Sports**, I've been to all of these sites.

So load up the family car, hit the road and get ready to soak up some Sunshine State sports.

Chip Carter
FOX13 Sports Director

SUNSHINE STATE SPORTS ATTRACTIONS
Major League Baseball
www.majorleaguebaseball.com

Florida Marlins, Pro Player Stadium, Fort Lauderdale
Tampa Bay Devil Rays, Tropicana Field, St. Petersburg

Spring Training Exhibition Baseball (Grapefruit League)

Atlanta Braves, Disney's Wide World of Sports, Kissimmee
Baltimore Orioles, Fort Lauderdale Stadium, Fort Lauderdale
Boston Red Sox, City of Palms Park, Fort Myers
Cincinnati Reds, Ed Smith Stadium, Sarasota
Cleveland Indians, Chain of Lakes Park, Winter Haven
Detroit Tigers, Marchant Stadium, Lakeland
Florida Marlins, Space Coast Stadium, Viera-Melbourne
Houston Astros, Osceola County Stadium, Kissimmee
Kansas City Royals, Baseball City Stadium, Davenport
Los Angeles Dodgers, Dodgertown, Vero Beach

Montreal Expos, Municipal Stadium, West Palm Beach
New York Mets, St. Lucie County Stadium, Port St. Lucie
New York Yankees, Legends Field, Tampa
Philadelphia Phillies, Jack Russell Memorial Stadium, Clearwater
Pittsburgh Pirates, McKechnie Field, Bradenton
Tampa Bay Devil Rays, Florida Power Park, St. Petersburg
Texas Rangers, Charlotte County Stadium, Port Charlotte
Toronto Blue Jays, Dunedin Stadium, Dunedin

Women's Professional Softball League
Tampa Bay Firestix, University of South Florida Softball Complex, Tampa

National Basketball Association - NBA.COM
Orlando Magic, Orlando Arena, Orlando
Miami Heat, American Airlines Arena, Miami

Women's National Basketball Association - WNBA.COM
Orlando Miracle, Orlando Arena, Orlando

National Football League - NFL.com
Tampa Bay Buccaneers, Raymond James Stadium, Tampa
Jacksonville Jaguars, Alltel Stadium, Jacksonville
Miami Dolphins, Pro Player Stadium, Fort Lauderdale

Arena Football League
Tampa Bay Storm, Ice Palace, Tampa
Orlando Predators, Orlando Arena, Orlando

National Hockey League - NHL.com
Tampa Bay Lightning, Ice Palace, Tampa
Florida Panthers, National Car Rental Center, Miami

Major League Soccer - www.mlsnet.com
Tampa Bay Mutiny, Raymond James Stadium, Tampa

NASCAR and International Racing-NASCAR.com
Daytona International Speedway, Daytona
Homestead-Miami Speedway, Homestead
Sebring International Raceway, Sebring

Division I College Athletics
Bethune-Cookman University, Daytona Beach
Florida A&M University, Tallahassee
Florida State University, Tallahassee
University of Central Florida, Orlando
University of Florida, Gainesville
University of Miami, Coral Gables
University of South Florida, Tampa

INDEX

A great way to travel is in your new Chrysler or Jeep. Visit your Chrysler and Jeep dealers today.

Alan Jay Chrysler-Plymouth-Jeep 5330 U.S. 27 S. Sebring, FL 33870 (941) 382-1177

B.M. Smith Motors 1722 S. Collins St. Plant City, FL 33566 (813) 752-5167

Courtesy Chrysler-Jeep 1728 W. Brandon Blvd. Brandon, FL 33511 (813) 685-4511

UAG Citrus Chrysler-Plymouth-Jeep 12020 U.S. 301 Dade City, FL 33525 (352) 521-0055

Country Jeep 14240 Cortez Blvd. Brooksville, FL 34613 (352) 597-0035

Crystal Chrysler-Plymouth 1601 W. Main St. Inverness, FL 34450 (352) 726-1238

Crystal Jeep 1005 S. Suncoast Blvd. Homosassa, FL 34448 (352) 563-2277

Dayton Andrews Chrysler-Plymouth-Jeep 2388 Gulf-to-Bay Blvd. Clearwater, FL 33765 (727) 799-4539

Ferman Chrysler-Plymouth-Jeep of New Port Richey 3939 U.S. 19 New Port Richey, FL 34652 (727) 847-5555

Ferman Chrysler-Plymouth-Jeep 1307 W. Kennedy Blvd. Tampa, FL 33606 (813) 253-2100

Ferman Chrysler-Plymouth-Jeep 11001 N. Florida Ave. Tampa, FL 33612 (813) 371-2600

Ferman of Wauchula 1401 U.S. 17 S. Wauchula, FL 33873 (941) 773-4744

Firkins Chrysler-Plymouth-Jeep 2700 First St. Bradenton, FL 34208 (941) 748-6510

Fitzgerald's Countryside Auto Mall 27365 U.S. 19 N. Clearwater, FL 33761 (727) 799-1800

Gettel Jeep of Sarasota 3480 Bee Ridge Road Sarasota, FL 34239 (941) 923-1411

Lakeland Chrysler-Plymouth 2335 U.S. 98 N. Lakeland, FL 33805 (941) 687-2501

Nichols Jeep 2382 S. Tamiani Trail Venice, FL 34293 (941) 484-8300

Plaza Chrysler-Plymouth 14358 Cortez Blvd. Brooksville, FL 34613 (352) 597-1265

Regal Jeep 2615 Lakeland Hills Blvd. Lakeland, FL 33805 (941) 687-8000

Sarasota Chrysler-Plymouth 6826 S. Tamiani Trail Sarasota, FL 34231 (941) 922-0711

St. Petersburg Chrysler-Plymouth-Jeep 2500 34th St. N. St. Petersburg, FL 33713 (727) 323-2000

Steve Sorensen Chrysler-Plymouth-Jeep 1900 U.S. 27 N. Lake Wales, FL 33853 (941) 676-0733

Suncoast Chrysler-Plymouth-Jeep 8755 Park Blvd. Seminole, FL 34642 (727) 393-4621

Tom Edwards 1425 W. Main St. Bartow, FL 33830 (941) 533-0793

Venice Chrysler-Plymouth 1550 S. Tamiani Trail Venice, FL 34293 (941) 493-5204

Wells Motor Company 1600 U.S. 27 S. Avon Park, FL 33825 (941) 453-6644

Winter Haven Chrysler-Plymouth-Jeep 190 Avenue "K" S.W. Winter Haven, FL 33880 (941) 299-1243

For travel convenience, check eroo.com

THERE'S ONLY ONE

Your One Hop Personal Stop™